SOLID STEPS To HAPPINESS &

SUCCESS

THINK RIGHT ~ DO RIGHT ~ BE RIGHT!

Edward Spade

Edward Spade

DEDICATION

To my parents, **John and Nora**, who have always been there to help and encourage me to do what is right no matter how good or bad the circumstances may have been. They are truly worth my honor.

I Love You Both!

To my lovely wife, **Cassie**, who is one of the kindest and most caring people I have ever met. She has continued to love me at times when my behavior and words have been unforgivable.

I Love You!

To my Great children:
Eddie ~ Olivia ~ & Timothy
Each of you will always have a special place in my Heart and Mind.

I Love You All!

CONTENTS

Edward Spade

ACKNOWLEDGMENTS

My Lord & Savior Jesus Christ

God the Son - who came to this earth, lived a perfect and sinless life, was **crucified for our sins**, according to the scriptures, **was buried**, and **rose again the third day**, as the Victor over sin, death, and the grave!

For all **have sinned**, and **come short** of the glory of God;
Romans 3:23

For the wages of sin is **death**; but the **gift of God is eternal life through Jesus Christ our Lord.**
Romans 6:23

And whosoever was not found written in the book of life was **cast into the lake of fire**.
Revelation 20:15

But **God** commendeth **his love** toward us, in that, while we were yet sinners, **Christ died for us**.
Romans 5:8

If you want to be saved/born-again you must come to **THE LORD JESUS CHRIST** and Confess Yourself as the Sinner that He **Died, was Buried, and Rose Again** for, the sinner for whom He **paid the penalty**, and **TRUST HIM** as Your Personal SAVIOR!

That if thou shalt **confess with thy mouth the Lord Jesus**, and shalt **believe in thine heart** that God hath raised him from the dead, thou shalt be **saved**.
Romans 10:9

For with the heart man **believeth unto righteousness**; and with the mouth confession is made unto **salvation**.
Romans 10:10

For whosoever shall **call upon the name of the Lord** shall be **saved**.
Romans 10:13

Happiness and Success

Far too many people waste time trying to buy happiness when it's readily available without costing a cent. Some people just wish and dream of a day when they'll be able to afford the things they think will make them happy and successful, like a new home, exotic vacations, and more.

Happiness and success isn't derived from tangible items. It's a state of mind that allows you to further your progress in both your personal and professional life so that every day, you're achieving goals and reaching new milestones toward a better life.

To get yourself into this state of mind, you have to develop daily habits that don't hold you back, but instead help you get more done during the day, meet obligations with ease, and lie down at night with a smile on your face because everything is headed in the right direction.

Account for Your Future

Your life is happening now. It's being lived whether or not you're in control. Each day and night that you wake up and go to bed is 24 hours of time that has passed by. For some people, those 24 hours really didn't amount to anything special except the passage of time.

For others, they accomplished something that brought them happiness and added to the success that they envision for themselves. The difference in these two types of people is that one lets life just happen to him, and the other plans and directs his own life.

Every day that you have to live is a day that you can control whether or not you're happy - whether or not you're going to be successful. It begins with a plan and is followed by action. What are you going to do today to take steps that create happiness?

What steps are you going to take to be successful? If you don't know what steps to take, then you have no course of action. If that sounds like something you've struggled with, you can learn how to account for your future.

By doing this, you will start planning ahead for what you want – and making it happen. You can plan ahead each day for how you're going to spend your time. Even your free time (and you should have free time) can be planned so that you're living a life that's full of happiness.

Planning ahead is one thing that the world's most successful people have in common. They don't fly by the seat of their pants and let things just happen – they plan the kind of life that they want to live.

They know that time is a precious commodity – perhaps one of the most valuable things to consider. They invest it wisely, just like they do the money they earn. Most people are great at investing in the lives of others.

You spend time doing things that bring happiness to people. You work hard to make others successful - whether those people are your work relationships or your personal ones.

There's nothing wrong with investing in others.

However, you need to learn how to invest in yourself and your own life. If you don't, you're actually withdrawing from your accounts of happiness and success instead of making deposits.

Without working on your happiness and success, it will be a long, hard struggle to get what you want - if you get it at all. Some people make plans well into the future, and others do it in smaller increments.

You might plan for something you want to achieve for happiness and success for the next day, next month or even the next year. But have an idea of how you want your day to unfold. Be specific, not vague – that way, you have a way to measure whether or not the day was a "win" for you.

Picture the Realization of Your Dreams

Learning to picture the realization of your dreams is a way to visualize what it is that you want. When you use visualization, you keep your focus on your goals instead of the obstacles. This works to keep you motivated. Studies have shown that motivated people are happier and less stressed than those who aren't.

It's also true that people who have a dream they want to accomplish find more inner satisfaction. The daily act of taking the time to picture your dreams leads you to appreciate the journey.

You will be able to find happiness - even when things go wrong - if whatever steps you're taking focus on seeing your dreams come true. Close your eyes and visualize you decorating your new home, seeing your bank account with a specific amount of money in it, or being welcomed home with open arms by a loving family.

This act of imagination will help you start living the role of the life you want to be in. But you don't want to stay chained to disappointment for what hasn't manifested itself yet.

Being appreciative of your current situation and where you're heading is important, too. Be grateful for the things and the opportunities that come your way that allow you to chase after what you want.

If you have good health that allows you to do what you want to do, be thankful for that. Whenever opportunities come along, recognize them for what they are, a step toward the future you want.

Even when obstacles show up, appreciate them. Because obstacles mean that you're moving forward and you're taking action to make the picture of your dreams become a reality.

Find a Daily Challenge

When you challenge yourself in any area of your life, you end up growing. If you stick to what you already know and you only do the things you know you're good at, you stay stagnant.

Choose an area of your life to challenge yourself in (and make sure that you cover each of them). For example, in the area of exercise, challenge yourself to do more than you thought you could with your exercise program.

Maybe instead of doing 30 minutes of walking each day, you increase it to 45 minutes. You will gain a sense of accomplishment that will make you feel both happy and successful.

Try a new food - something that's outside of your comfort zone. This broadens your horizons and can help you learn about other cultures. Maybe you find happiness in cooking, so this can bring your family together, too.

Learn something new. People that continually grow in knowledge challenge their brain. This can be a new language, book, or skill. It could be something like taking an online course or visiting a place that moves you, shakes up your life, and gives you a deeper perspective.

Resurrect a failure. Every single person in the world has a failure of some kind in their life. They tried something and it didn't work. They couldn't accomplish a goal -

couldn't grasp enough of the knowledge needed to make an idea work.

Look back over something that you tried and really wanted but gave up on. Sometimes the passing of time can add fresh ideas and a better understanding of why the failure happened.

When you look back over your life at something that failed, it could be that you just weren't prepared for that success. When you challenge yourself to be an "overcomer", you will find a sense of happiness because of the completion of each task.

Finishing something contributes to success. It's especially rewarding when you go back to something you previously failed at. Remember, it took many tries before the lightbulb finally worked!

Make It a Point to Give Every Day Your All

We all have areas of life that we hold back in. Maybe it comes out of fear of looking stupid, or fear of failure. But working hard every single day is the key to success.

In everything that you put your hand to, you have to give it your all. If it's working around your house, don't settle for "good enough". Keep going - and even if you have to start the task all over again, work hard to make it right.

But remember - there is a difference in doing a task right and being a perfectionist. You can give your all with work and in personal relationships, and when you see the difference between doing enough and doing as much as you can, it will shock you at how much better things are when you try hard.

Be fully present in everything you do every single day. Refuse to let yourself go through life on autopilot. You can tell if you're on autopilot if you finish doing something, but you can't remember parts about doing the task.

Your body was there working, but your mind was already off on something else. When you're fully present, it can give you an appreciation for what you're doing and for what you have.

Some people call this mindfulness others call it being in the now. You leave multi- tasking behind and focus on one thing at a time – one conversation, one meal, one project, etc. It helps you maximize your effort and emerge with better results than if you didn't try as hard.

Stop Working When It's Time to Stop

Remember that your life is a series of seconds, minutes and hours each day. It's important to work hard because this contributes to your happiness and success. There's nothing wrong with being the kind of person who works hard.

But if you're working so many hours and you have such big projects on your shoulders that the line between work and your free time is blurred, it's time to take a step back.

There's a reason that taking time off work is important. This helps you recharge your batteries and helps you relax and not lose sight of the big picture of your life. Work is only a portion of your life. There are other aspects to it. When you allow work to take over, it throws everything else out of balance. This is one of the reasons that people start to eat unhealthy meals when they're working too hard.

They get too tired or too stressed to take the time to prepare a healthy meal. It's easier to grab whatever is convenient. If they took the time to de-stress, they would be making healthier decisions that would serve their work better.

You will be happier if you set work boundaries. People that have a definitive line between their work and off time are far more successful. When you take time off, you can actually improve your work performance.

Not doing this will lead to unhappiness, poor health, stress and can negatively affect your intimate relationships. Besides, you need to enjoy the fruits of your labor, and having a predetermined quitting time will enable you to make plans for that!

Protect Your Sleep Time

Striving to find personal satisfaction - especially if you're trying to build a business - can impact your sleep. You might already know the importance of getting the sleep that your body needs.

But what you might not know is that when you skip out on getting enough sleep, you can sabotage yourself. Losing sleep leads to feelings of unhappiness, anxiety and irritability.

Plus, when you don't get the sleep that your body needs, it leads to a loss of productivity. You will begin to slow down physically and cognitively because your body just can't function at top performance when it doesn't have the right amount of sleep.

You will find articles and advice that will tell you that you must get at least eight hours of sleep every night in order for it to be enough for your body. But the truth is that eight hours can be too much for some people and not enough for others.

One way to tell if you're getting the right amount of sleep for your body can be determined by how you feel in the mornings. If you wake up and you feel refreshed, that's a sign that you're getting enough sleep.

Feeling sluggish means that you're not getting the right amount. Getting enough sleep replaces the energy reserves that you drained during the day. If you fail to refill them, then you're running on a deficit the next day.

Sometimes the unhappiness in our personal lives or the work stress will prevent a good night's sleep. It's a vicious cycle, because a lack of sleep contributes to the same issues.

If you're not sleeping enough, start by examining your sleep habits. Are you getting to bed early enough? Are you sleeping in a cool room with no distractions? Is your bedding comfortable? Is there light in your room?

Make sure you get to the root cause of the issue, because sleep is one health habit that will interfere with every part of your life, making you miserable – and possibly making you take out your frustrations on others.

Make Exercise and Eating Right a Priority

Having a daily habit of exercising can create happiness. When you exercise, your body releases endorphins or the feel good hormones that can lift your mood. When you exercise every day - even if it's just going for a walk around the block at work or at home - you help improve the way your organs can do their jobs.

You make it easier for them to function. You also create more mental alertness in your brain when you exercise, because you increase the way that your organs can get the oxygen that they need.

Not getting enough oxygen can negatively affect your organs - and that includes your brain. Without the right amount of oxygen, it can impair your ability to think and to work through ideas, to attain goals and to get done what you want to get done each day.

But when you exercise, you create a way for your whole body to benefit - and this produces a sense of happiness. Making sure that you eat right can go a long way toward creating happiness and success in your life, too.

When you eat the wrong kinds of food, it can have an impact on how you feel physically and how you feel mentally. For example, there are certain foods that zap your energy.

When you eat them, you feel tired as your energy levels crash. If you eat a lot of foods that are high on the glycemic index, you will experience fatigue. This will affect your performance because the tiredness will make it harder for you to concentrate.

Fatty foods, sugary foods and high carb foods should be eaten in moderation. Think of food as your body's fuel to propel you through the day where you can get the most done on your "want to do" list.

Dress Successfully Every Day

The way that you dress affects your self-esteem and can make you feel less or more confident. Wearing clothes that are ill fitting or unflattering can affect your happiness.

You can even feel anxious or depressed. The clothing that you wear presents an image to the world - but the most important image is the one that *you* see. If you're someone who battles self-esteem and confidence issues, wearing clothes that feed into that will subtract from your happiness.

You can try an experiment. Wear a pair of worn out sweatpants and a baggy shirt out in public. Don't take the time to fix your hair. Then go out wearing a nice outfit with your hair attractively styled.

You will notice a difference in the way that you walk and in the way that you act. When you dress like it doesn't matter, it will change how you see yourself. But more than that, it changes how you will handle what you want to do that day.

You won't feel your sharpest because the clothes affect you mentally. You don't have to spend a lot of money to dress for success. What a lot of people don't realize is that dressing for success isn't just referring to looking the part.

It's referring to internal feelings, too. When you dress for success, you feel happier. You feel like a success and then your actions will follow those feelings. Make it a habit every day to dress in clothes that make you feel good about yourself.

If you're working online and having to present yourself to an audience via video, or meeting with people in person, dressing for success can help present a more professional image, which can boost your sales, in turn – making you happier!

Don't try to implement a bunch of new daily habits all at once. Build slowly. It takes awhile for a new habit to take root, so don't beat yourself up if you're slow to implement them on a routine basis.

It takes a few weeks to get with the program, but you will start to notice positive changes and that will motivate you to continue each and every day.

Mental Training

There's a psychology that can help people learn how to focus mentally to gain better performance. When getting what you want out of life is important to you, you can use your mental ability to achieve your goals.

With mental training, you can accomplish great things. You can learn how to structure your time so that you stay focused on what needs to be done. You will gain the ability to recognize which jobs need to be done and which ones are just wasting your time.

You will also be able to eliminate the mental roadblocks that can keep you from going where you want to be in life. Using mental training increases your focus. When you begin a job, you will be able to complete it with fewer distractions.

You will gain a greater sense of achievement and completion ratio than you had in the past. What does it mean to engage in mental training? It's similar to working out your muscles – you're training your mind to be tough and perform for you.

Know What You Really Want

There are far too many people working hard to go after achievements in life that they really don't even want. For some of these people, they're following the advice of a family member or friend.

They're allowing what someone else thinks is best to govern their lives. While everyone can benefit from advice, it's not beneficial if deep down, it's not really what motivates you.

Your core beliefs will cause you to work towards the life that you want. If, deep down, you're telling yourself you're never going to succeed, then you will make sure that comes true.

What would your life be like if there were no obstacles and you could have the life you dreamed of having – in the niche that made you extremely happy? This isn't about winning the lottery and never working again – it's about knowing what provides satisfaction in your mind.

You can't be excited about performance in any area of your life if it's not something that you're passionate about. Passion creates motivation. Motivation gets you going.

When you're motivated about something, you can't wait to approach it. Passion and motivation work together to make things happen. This is true for both your personal and professional life.

Motivation fuels the drive within you and causes you to give everything you've got to a project. Knowing what you really want allows you to look for opportunities to do things that you enjoy.

It helps you learn to say no to even potentially good things if they're not something that you're passionate about. When you really want something, it's easier to keep your motivation and your energy level up.

It's easier to keep on going in the face of difficulties or setbacks. When you have a passion for something that stems from going after what you really want, you won't stop until you find a way to achieve it.

When you care about something, it causes you to give it your all - to do the best possible job that you can. It's the opposite when you don't care about something. You just want to get that task over with using as little energy and effort as possible.

Knowing what you really want makes it easier for your mind to come up with creative solutions and ideas to make your passions succeed. It unleashes a deeper problem-solving mentality.

Before you wake up and start going through the motions in your personal or professional life, decide what it is that you truly want and then you can focus your mental energy on making it happen.

Become very aware of every benefit regarding what it is you're aiming for in life. Seeing those benefits mapped out can give you strength to continue through difficult times and reach the finish line.

Don't just say what goals you have. List why you have those goals – how achieving them would better your life – what it would personally mean to you when it comes true.

Mental Training Gives You Confidence

There is no one in the world that is 100% confident all of the time. We all have areas in life where self-doubt creeps in and tries to tear down ideas or destroy dreams.

It's important that you have the mental training that gives you the confidence to put your goals into action. There are negative statements in each of us. These are phrases designed to keep you from succeeding - or in some cases, from even trying.

You might be living with a negative mental teleprompter that feeds you lines that destroy your confidence. This can cause you to have a battle that you can't afford to engage in.

This negative mental attitude can damage your peak performance by causing you anxiety, depression - and even convincing you to give up. You need confidence on your side.

If your inner voice is feeding you lines such as, "You can't do that" or, "You don't have the skills, talent, or money to accomplish this," then it's time that you shut it down.

What this negative self-talk is doing is poisoning the soil of your mind so that you don't aim for peak performance because mentally, you've already lost the battle – *and the war.*

This kind of self-talk gets you to picture what can never be (anything good) or what you want (happiness and success) because you don't deserve it. It's time to silence that inner voice by correcting these false mental statements.

When you hear, "You can't do that" in your mind, you need to zap that statement and then give it the boot. Picture opening a door labeled, "I can" and kicking the negative "You can't" right out of your mind.

This requires some mental training to do this. Don't give your negativity an audience. Have some fortitude and continue to visualize giving the negative statement the boot for good.

Retrain your mind with positive thoughts about yourself and what is possible. Replace every negative statement with a positive one, immediately. It takes practice to recognize when you're being a downer to yourself.

If you have a setback, it's not that you blew it. You just have to find another way. How you work in life and what you can accomplish will be settled within you long before you even make the first attempt.

Don't allow yourself to dwell on any thought that stands in the way of your dreams because you deserve for them to come true. The mind is a tool that you can use to accomplish any task - whether it's mental, emotional or physical.

Over time, as you implement the practice of positive self talk, you will notice that this becomes your new way of automatically viewing things – in a positive light. You won't even have to try hard anymore – it just happens.

Train yourself to see the opportunities in every failure. This is a chance to learn and grow stronger. It's almost like how we tear down muscles in order for them to grow back – bigger and stronger with every workout.

There's a lot of discomfort in failure. But mental training means you sit there and learn how to tolerate that feeling without quitting. Feel uncomfortable – it won't kill you. Calmly practice working through those moments with calm clarity instead of frustration and panic.

Develop Mental Clarity

Sometimes new ideas or opportunities can come at you in warp speed. That's because we live life in the fast lane and that's not likely to change. But it does mean that you have to be ready to grab the chances that come your way.

Life is not a yes or no experience. It's more multiple choice. You won't be presented with simply one choice or one route to take in life. Instead, you will get hundreds of choices that come your way every day of your life.

These choices that you make will decide whether you experience success or suffer through a setback. Sometimes we make choices based on what we're focusing all of our mental energy on.

We can become so focused on accomplishing something a certain way or before a certain time that we close our mind off to any other options. This means a different opportunity - a better one - can get overlooked.

You should always take the time to develop mental clarity about every move that you make in life. Don't allow yourself to be led by your emotions and don't make snap decisions.

If you're presented with an opportunity that requires immediate action, you will want to be careful that if you take this action, it keeps you on the track you want to be on.

Some opportunities really are a pot of gold at the end of the rainbow and if you travel toward them, you will get success. But others only have an empty journey that takes us farther away from what we intended on doing.

Check every idea and every opportunity to be sure that it lines up with your plan - that you don't have to lower your morals or change who you are to grasp the chance.

It's better to remain true to who you are and the vision that you have for your life than to be misled by too good to be true opportunities that can affect what you really want.

This is why it's important to have goals. Goals can help give you clarity when things become less clear to you. You can check every opportunity that arises against your goals.

Every opportunity that you take should bring you closer to your overall end result. If it doesn't, then it could be a wasted experience. Having mental clarity can help you get in touch with your inner self and quiet the chatter that comes with living in this digital age.

It can let you see whether or not you're engaging in peak performance in how you're managing all areas of your life. Clarity comes from being mindful and knowing what you want. Practice making thoughtful decisions and get in the habit of living life from a clear perspective.

Make Your Move

It's important to know what you want and to have mental clarity, but without a plan of action, you won't make progress. You have to take the time to understand each course of action that you engage in.

You need goals and you need a good strategy in both your personal and professional life. But then you need to push forward and give the action that you undertake everything you've got.

Each step that you take on your journey to personal success leads you to the next one. You can't get where you want to be and meet those goals without making a move.

Plenty of people have good ideas. They make a list of goals that are designed to bring their ideas, their wants, and their dreams to reality. They have an excellent strategy in place for pulling everything together. But then they wait.

They wait until the "perfect" opportunity or the "right" time before they make their move. The problem with this is that first, there are no perfect opportunities and secondly, procrastination is the killer of action.

When you're procrastinating, you're not moving forward and you run out of steam. When you fall into the trap of "I was going to, but..." you run the risk that you will never see the end result of your dreams or your goals.

What you wanted out of life will pass you by and as you grow older, you will have plenty of regrets. Make sure that you look over what it is that you want in life and do something to move forward in that direction.

Even if it's a small something that you take action with, it's progress. Make your move mentally before you make your move physically. In all of the actions that you need to complete to make what you want possible, you have to realize what you're capable of and what you can't handle.

If you want to run a business and you have no idea about record keeping, payroll, accounting and all of the financial wisdom that comes along with that area, then take the action of finding someone who does.

You don't gain the mental training overnight that leads to peak performance. You develop it. You work it out. When you take action, you're transferring that mental training from the mental to the physical.

It's much easier to carry out the actual task if you allow yourself the mental run- through of seeing it proceed into fruition. You can optimize your performance by doing whatever it is that gets you ready.

Do whatever it is that gives you the unwavering focus that you need. Some people read back over their life's mission statement. Others engage in a habit, such as reading empowering quotes or words to get themselves mentally charged up to act.

Mental training to take action often relies on putting yourself out there and making a commitment publicly. For others, that would be uncomfortable, so the commitment might be made to themselves only.

Engage yourself in exercises to fortify your focus and become an action-taker. Use a timer on your smart phone to record your progress with each task. Whenever you realize you've been distracted and are off course, stop the timer.

Find out how often you stop doing tasks and start avoiding things because you've become your #1 obstacle in your professional life.

Mental Training to Mental Toughness

Being mentally tough is having a no quit attitude. It's a determination or psychological strength to succeed even when life doesn't go the way that you feel it should.

You need this kind of mental toughness in all areas of life. Getting what you want out of life isn't something that happens to those who aren't mentally tough. That's because setbacks and failures are going to happen.

Mental training can create an iron will in you to keep you going through tough circumstances, to achieve a goal or reach a dream regardless of what's standing in the way.

You need mental training in many areas - but especially in the area of change. This is because people tend to think of goals or life plans as being all or nothing. They don't plan for any contingencies because they don't foresee it.

Or they don't want something to go wrong so badly that they're afraid planning for it will make a plan fail. So they don't. There's a saying that says, "If you fail to plan, you plan to fail," so adhere to that statement instead of worrying that if you make a plan for failure, it might come true.

Rarely does any goal or plan work out 100% the way that you want it or expect it to. Knowing how to adjust a goal is for your benefit. This way, you can take on a setback and it doesn't knock you out of the competition for good.

You stay in the game - you just utilize a new idea of how to get that goal accomplished. With mental training, you learn to understand that success is not something that you arrive at and then you're done.

Success is always changing. It's the here and now that matters most - not the future. This can help you see the importance in having goals that reflect your current life, not ones that you made in the past that don't take into account who or where you are today.

Mental training helps you see that you must be confident and strive for what you want each day - that you have to be thankful for the journey instead of being so focused on the end result that you miss out on all of the chances and opportunities and good things all around you right now.

If you keep your focus solely on a goal you didn't make, you can miss opportunities that could translate into even better things for your life. This is where you have to be mentally tough enough to learn what you need to let go of and what you need to hold on to.

Some opportunities will shift and change. You will have to recognize when something is no longer serving a purpose or helping to meet an end result. This mental toughness is needed to make changes that can be difficult, such as ending a business relationship when it's not helping you reach personal success.

Or it might be leaving a personal relationship that's holding you back from being your best self. These decisions shouldn't be taken lightly, but they shouldn't be ignored either, just because they make you uncomfortable.

Find Your Catalyst

A catalyst can be something that you experience - such as an event, or it can be words spoken by another person, a book or a movie that causes you to change your life in some way.

Some catalysts are simple - such as a man who gets fired because he's always late. Losing the job can be a catalyst for that man to make sure he gets to his next job on time, or find a job that gives him so much personal satisfaction, he never wants to let his company down.

The event of getting fired, often at an inopportune time, caused him to make a change in how he acts in life. Change can be difficult. It's easier to do what you've always done because there's comfort in that which you are familiar with.

Leaving your comfort zone puts you into new situations and forces you to deal with new ideas and new ways of handling various aspects of life. It's scary and usually no one wants to go through it voluntarily.

If you were to take a survey of random strangers and ask them, "Are you happy with your life?" you would get more "no" answers than you would "yes" ones. There are a lot of people who aren't happy with their lives.

They don't like their personal life or their professional life - and they don't like how they act sometimes. Yet day in and day out, they don't do anything to change any of that.

Some people don't know how to change it. They don't understand how they can find a catalyst to motivate and inspire themselves toward the kind of life they want.

Sometimes a catalyst enters your life, and you're too focused on the ordinary, that you miss it completely. You may have to train yourself to watch for opportunities if you want to raise yourself to a higher level of success and happiness.

Change Begins and Ends with You

If you take the time to look over your life at this moment, what would you think about it? Think about the people in your life - those who you have an intimate relationship with.

Is it everything you wanted it to be and hoped it could be? What about where you are financially in life? Does where you stand right now with your finances make you wish things were different?

Does it create a hunger within you to have more? To be wiser about your finances? What about your job? This is an area where a lot of people are absolutely miserable.

Yet, they stay in that job year after year getting older and even more miserable. If you dislike any area of your life because it simply isn't satisfying you, but you stick with it anyway, it means that you've settled.

You've given up on the idea that there could be more - that you deserve more or that changing things is even worth the effort. If you dislike an area of your life now, but you don't change anything about it, you will still dislike that area of your life three months, six months or a year down the road.

You will have lost time and you will have missed the opportunity to make changes during that timeframe. If you want more out of life - if you feel that you should have more - and the unhappiness with your life sits like a rock in the pit of your stomach, then you need to take steps to make changes.

Physical signs like that are always indicators that something isn't the way you want it to be – that it needs to be addressed. And ignoring these physical signs can lead to emotional complications as the stress of the matter weighs heavily on you.

Remaining where you are in a life you're not happy with will lead to feelings of anger, depression, sadness and resignation. That hole inside of you that aches for something more, for something better will never be filled.

That's not what you deserve. It's not what anyone deserves. Life is not meant to be something that's just endured. It's meant to be lived with excitement because it's an adventure if you decide that it is.

Roadblocks That Get in Your Way

Though people are all different, we all have one thing in common - roadblocks that get in the way of what we really want from life. Roadblocks stop some people from ever making a change, but they motivate others to keep on going to find a way to what they want, regardless of the roadblock.

You might have one of these roadblocks or you might experience more than one of them. A major roadblock to change is fear. When things change, it brings in differences that can make us afraid.

We're afraid to leave behind the bad job for fear we won't like the new one - fear that we might not fit in as well. Remember though, that one of the acronyms for fear is False Evidence Appearing Real.

Your fears are usually based on what if myths - and they almost always never come to pass. Don't let fear cause you to sit on the sidelines of change. Another roadblock that gets in the way is a lack of knowledge.

It's hard to make changes when you're not sure exactly how to go about those changes. You might be branching out into an area that's completely beyond your scope of knowledge at the present time.

Remember that what you don't know can be learned. Use educational resources as your catalyst for change and success. Strive for new levels of insight that you previously didn't have.

Thinking that you simply can't add another activity to your already full life keeps many people stuck where they are. Making changes requires work. So many people see the effort as not worth the payoff - and that's a mistake.

This belief is what keeps you rooted to the job that you hate, to those messy finances, or to that relationship that's sucking the life right out of you. Learning better time management skills can be a catalyst for a better life as you clear out things that are a waste of time and make room for what offers the most benefits.

Being just comfortable enough where you are can be a roadblock to motivate you not to change. You are not 100% happy, but you are "happy enough." All this means is that you settled for a life that keeps you locked into your comfort zone.

You are trading a full life for one that's half empty - because if you're not 100% satisfied, then something is missing. That something may be the very thing that you always wanted, but because you were "happy enough," you will never reach it.

Visualization can be a catalyst for the changes you need to make. Picture the next level of success in every area of your life – spiritually, mentally, emotionally, physically, financially, relationships, health – everything that matters most to you.

Focus on how it could be improved and then make a game plan to get you there. If you block out those thoughts in an effort to stay content, you will never know what you could have made out of your life if you'd give it a chance.

Wanting everything to be perfect is a huge roadblock to motivation. It's here where people stall out. They want the new situation to be perfect before they attempt any changes.

They want the new job to have everything in place. They don't want to take the chance that they'll make a switch and find it's not what they wanted. These are people who wait for the "perfect" relationship before getting into one.

Perfectionism is the killer of change because what you see in your mind as perfection doesn't translate that way in life. That's because there are no perfect scenarios in a life that's lived to the fullest.

There are experiences to encounter – and not one of them will be perfect. That's okay. Perfectionism kills progress. You don't want to be sitting on the sidelines waiting to get into the game of life.

The number one roadblock that keeps too many people from letting a catalyst be their motivation is the fear of failure. They falsely believe that they haven't failed yet because they haven't even tried – so they're safe.

But whether they realize it or not, they *have* failed. They're choosing to stay stagnant in a lesser life than what they dreamed of. That, in itself, is a form of failure.

Another roadblock happens when people wait for change rather than seeking change. They wait for the perfect joint venture partner to come to them instead of seeking one out, because that requires putting themselves on the line.

They wait to see if the person they're in a relationship with is going to treat them better, rather than speaking up about what they want and deserve. They avoid tough situations and tough conversations because they're waiting for everything to work out on its own.

Change isn't something that happens on a whim. It's something that you *make* happen. You have to find the motivation within yourself to make that change. And it's uncomfortable at first.

That's okay. Take that sign of discomfort as a compliment. It's proving to you that you're taking action and bettering your life, even in the face of fear or uneasiness.

Your Mind Can Be a Catalyst

You get the life that you think you deserve. Your mind can lead you to make changes - to take action that alters the life you currently have. What usually happens when someone's mind leads them to take action is they become so upset with their current situation, they think leaving it where it's at is no longer an option.

Their emotions will often reach a point that they must make a change. This drive can often start out backed by an emotion. For example, if someone is in a relationship with a person who didn't treat them that well, they'll often stick with the relationship until a catalyst fueled by emotion causes a change.

One emotion could be anger. If the person you're in a relationship with is unfaithful, it's often anger over the cheating that drives the catalyst - even when the prior bad behavior didn't induce a change.

Your subconscious knows what you truly want. What happens is this true desire becomes buried deep under what we're willing to settle for. This is why so many people aren't living a life full of passion.

You can tell if you're living a life full of passion by asking yourself this question. Do I love getting out of bed in the morning? If you're not excited about what you get to do when you get out of bed, that's a warning sign that you need to find your catalyst.

Whatever it is that motivates you is what will drive you to wake up, ready to start and excel throughout your day. It will drive you to keep going in the face of obstacles.

You will continue on - even if you're the only one who believes in you, or your idea or your change. That's why it's vital to your success – to your ability to thrive - that you get into a business that you have a strong emotional attachment to – something you are proud of and believe in strongly.

Face the Truth

Did you ever hear of someone who had a terrible health scare because they made bad choices in life that led to the issue? It shook them up - and for awhile, they strictly followed the doctor's orders.

They ate right. They exercised. They got the correct amount of sleep that they needed. They quit smoking cigarettes. They quit drinking alcohol. Yet before several months passed, they slipped right back into their old habits.

The catalyst, which was the health scare, came face to face with personal responsibility - and lost. The hard truth is that in order for your catalyst to motivate you, you're going to have to accept personal responsibility.

The choices that you make in life are *your* choices. You made them because you thought they were the best option at the time. You might have received bad advice that led you to a decision - but in the end, you were the one that made that choice.

You have to accept personal responsibility for what you want to see changed in your life before it can change. People who place the blame on others for their lot in life don't ever reach a place where they're truly happy - regardless of the changes.

That's because they see life as happening *to* them rather than them making life happen. Accept the responsibility for your mistakes, for your poor choices, for that awful job you shouldn't have taken, or for that relationship that was a mess from the start that you wasted too much time on.

Once you accept it, you can move on. You can free yourself to finally accept the catalyst for change. Don't let where you were be a stone around your neck that anchors you to the place where you currently are.

Let the mistakes you made in the past become part of your motivation - part of your growing experience. While growth can be difficult, good things happen as you learn and utilize your lessons from the past and move to a different level in life.

5 Ways You Can Find Your Catalyst

Knowing that you want your life to change requires that you take stock of your life. It means that you have to examine every area and look at what's not been working to make you feel the inner happiness and success that you'd like to have.

The first way that you can find your catalyst is to understand the things in your life that matter to you. Your catalyst for motivation won't be the same as someone else's.

While what matters to one person may be an expensive house, that might not matter to you. Your priority might be financial security for your retirement, or more time to spend with your loved ones.

If having time to do what you want to do with creative work is what matters to you, then your catalyst will be whatever action gives you the chance to accomplish this.

This may be something as simple as cutting back on hours with work or finding a different job. It might be the catalyst of taking an art or a writing class. Whatever it is should be something that you truly desire - something that you feel your life would be lacking if you didn't have it.

The second way is to accept that you're going to have to change things in order to get what matters most to you. Many people are willing to acknowledge what matters to them, but then they fail to make any of the changes necessary to accomplish them.

You won't get what matters to you without change. It's like losing weight. You can't lose pounds if you stay idle and continue eating more food than necessary. You have to be mindful of your movement and intake.

The third way to find your catalyst is to give it the opportunity to happen. For example, if you want to start your own business, but your personal and professional life doesn't leave you with enough time to learn about business development or to increase your talents, then something has to go.

You have to make room to let the change in. Maybe that means spending a little time after work on the weekdays or on the weekends to educate yourself. It's a temporary sacrifice for a long-term benefit.

The fourth way to find your catalyst is to make it concrete. Write it down. Share it with others. Find a mentor. Don't allow this change you want to remain nothing more than a desire.

By naming it, you're taking a step toward making it your future reality. Decide what it is that you want for your life. Then make a sensible plan to go after it, step-by-step.

The fifth way is to not let the size of the change throw you off your goal. Some changes that people want to make are really big. Changes like moving from your home to live in another country because it's what you've always wanted is a huge change.

You wouldn't want to pack up overnight and head out the next morning. You can't throw away personal responsibility when a catalyst happens. What you have to do is focus on the things you need to do in order to reach that change sensibly.

If your goal is moving to another country, you would want to find a place to live and secure a way to support yourself financially before taking the leap. Those are action steps that you can take which will lead to the big change.

Small change is what equals big change and it gets you closer to where you want to be in life. Think about how often you've just accepted your fate – your lot in life.

Have you ever made an action plan to get to a better place? To have more peaceful relationships by setting boundaries? To feel the thrill of waking up each morning, ready to work on what excites you?

If you've been watching time pass by, waiting for a bolt of lightening, consider this day your wake up call. It's time to embrace every catalyst you encounter so that years down the road, you're not still stuck in the mud wondering why life passed you by.

Goal Setting Strategy

Everyone has certain goals they want to reach. It might be weight loss or finances in your personal life, or specific business growth goals in your career. Regardless of what milestones you want to achieve, you won't get there if all you have is the end result in mind.

Setting goals is just one part of the equation. Knowing how to get there is the piece of the puzzle that so many people leave out, which leads them to stumble, procrastinate and veer off course until one day they realize they're completely off base and have wasted a lot of time and effort.

There are four easy steps you can take to ensure your goals are met. It's a process that allows you to map out where you want to be and take steps to get there with ease.

Step 1 - Know Your End Result

In order to know what steps you need to take, you have to know how you'd like your journey to end. This is your outcome or end result. You have to be able to concretely define what you want that result to be.

This is the bottom line of everything that you're attempting to do. Many people aim for something without ever knowing what they want the end result to be. The problem with not knowing your end goal is that you won't realize it once you've reached it - if you even reach it at all.

Let's say that you take up running for the exercise. Your end result could be to lose weight or get in better shape. Now let's say that you set a more specific goal to take up running because you want to run in a marathon that's happening in the future.

Your end result changed from a generic goal of losing weight and getting in better shape to the end result of competing in the marathon, which has a specific length and is on a specific timetable.

Only you will be able to determine your end goal. It might be to finish college, grow your business by $100,000 in the coming year, lose 35 pounds, and so on. Have a large, verifiable goal to reach.

Knowing the end result is imperative for whatever it is that you want in life. You need to know this to be able to work your process. This might mean that you figure out different end results for different areas of your life.

It's okay to have one for the personal side of your life for relationships and things like that while having another one for your professional goals. Don't just say, "I want to be happier."

What would make you happier, specifically? Visualize the specific end goal that you want. For now, don't worry about timing. You will be working on that as you develop your specific goal setting strategy.

Step 2 - Craft Mini Goals

Goals are something that can be used to improve your life. By having goals, you can check to see if you're on track for how you want your life to turn out. Goals are helpful tools that can keep you headed in the right direction when you need to make a decision that involves changing some area of your life.

Encouragement is a by-product of having goals. Whenever you have a setback, goals can encourage you to keep going. By seeing how far you've already come, you realize that you've already made some forward progress.

Most success-minded people will focus on short-term goals over long-term goals because these are easier to make reality. Living in a results-oriented world causes people to lean toward short-term goals more often.

Dreamers who take very little action often focus on long-term goals, forgetting that they need a specific path to reach them. They stay paralyzed, feeling the long-term goal is too far out of their reach.

Having short-term goals means that these are things that you do in the present or in the very near future - such as within a week or a month. An example of a short- term goal might be setting up an email autoresponder system within the next 14 days so that you're ready to build a list.

A long-term goal is usually something that you can't reach as fast as a short term goal. A long-term goal is one that you plan to reach within a few months, a year or longer after making it.

Long-term goals will be realized over time as each of your shorter milestones are achieved. For instance, your long-term goal might be to have a list of 10,000 subscribers.

So your short-term goals might be:

Set up an email autoresponder system within 14 days Create a 10-day follow-up series for the autoresponders within 30 days Achieve a list of my first 200 subscribers using social media within 6 weeks Grow my list to 1,000 subscribers within 2 months using a giveaway event

...and so on.

Each time you're able to look at your list and cross off an item that you've achieved, it helps you build momentum toward reaching your ultimate goal. Whatever your goals are, you shouldn't let them just sit there as nothing more than an internal dream that you have.

You need them around visually so that they can help remind you of what you desire out of life. You need to be able to see whatever it is that your goals are so that you're reminded to take the necessary action.

You can create a vision board with pictures that will help keep you motivated. Or you can write them down in a notebook and list the reasons why you want to achieve that goal.

Studies have shown goals that are visualized or written down are reached more often than goals that are not. It moves you forward into doing all of the small steps needed to keep you climbing the ladder of success.

Reaching any goal will require you understanding what it is that you already possess that can help you meet that goal. It also takes you understanding what you lack in reaching that goal so that you can add it to your skills and achieve it.

If you wanted to run a marathon and you were in good shape, you would understand that your physical condition was something that you already had. But if you were out of shape, you would understand that you could not run a marathon until you got into the proper condition.

You would understand that you lacked the physical conditioning. Defining that would help you set mini goals of getting fit, so that would then feed into your larger goal of accomplishing the marathon.

You can dig down and create mini goals for as many sub-levels as you want, too. For example, physical conditioning is a mini goal to competing in the marathon. But what are some mini goals for the physical conditioning?

Being able to go the distance of the marathon in a day
Being able to run instead of walk the entire time
Being able to achieve a 7-minute mile or less

Creating mini goals helps you focus all of your energy on the bigger goal. Focusing solely on the bigger goal can make you feel overwhelmed and cause you to talk yourself out of trying.

Making mini goals takes the overall goal and reduces it in size so that it's manageable and very doable. You won't allow yourself to have excuses as to why it can't be achieved.

Each mini goal that you set needs to be specific, too. This means that you divide these up into tasks. You would need to use a calendar in order to set a date for reaching each task that falls under your mini goal heading.

You then break down the date by the time that you have to work on the goal. When you have goals that have a conclusion date, it helps you stay on track to reach the bigger picture.

Goals, even mini goals with a conclusion date of "whenever" rarely get finished. You need to know when you should start that mini goal and when it needs to be completed.

Give each task under the goal a deadline. For example, a mini goal of walking a 15 minute mile within 15 weeks might require you (if you're starting from a 30 minute mile) to shave one minute off your time each week.

That's a very doable mini goal, and the timeline is specific enough for you to have clarity in reaching it. Everything that you do under a mini goal should be something that matters. The more specific it is, the better it will be at keeping you on track.

Mini goals need to be created in such a way that you will be able to see progress. If your goal is to start your own business, then one of your mini goals might be to write a business plan.

Next, you would write down when you need that plan finished by. Another mini goal could be having a mentor look over the plan and give you tips on how to further improve it.

Each step that you take should have a purpose that moves you toward the end result of your bigger goal. If you can remove the mini goal without it impacting the overall goal, then odds are high that the mini goal may not be needed.

You need to have an order of importance in place before setting mini goals. After listing the mini goal, write down what you gain from reaching that goal. Write down what you need to do to complete it.

List the deadline that it needs to happen by. Make notes under the mini goal that tell you what you must learn to reach that goal. Is there a class you need to take? A book you have to read or a seminar you must attend?

All of those should be listed under the mini goal. Make sure that you understand if completing the mini goal can be done alone or if you're going to need someone else's help with it.

You should list all of the possible roadblocks that could happen during the course of trying to reach each mini goal. After you list the roadblocks, write down all of the ways around them.

What this does is help you be prepared for whenever a setback shows up. They will - and it's always best to have your offensive strategy in place before you need it.

Step 3 - Brainstorm Action Steps

Before you can take any action, you want to brainstorm ways to achieve your goals and mini goals. You want options, not just a single path that you think will work. It allows you to think outside the box.

Some people refer to brainstorming as creatively solving a problem before it happens or while it's ongoing. Without brainstorming, most people come up with between two and four ways that they can reach their goals.

When you start brainstorming from a research perspective, you often find better ways to do things, shortcuts and money savers. Don't be afraid to network with others and ask for their best practices, too.

Brainstorming action steps is easy to do. You need a notebook or computer. You start by thinking about the steps that you need to take and you just record whatever thoughts pop into your mind.

As you record your thoughts, you may start to see how some of them are connected and might possibly overlap one another. This will help you see how you may need to prioritize or even group certain action steps.

When you brainstorm, you are free thinking - and that can often let your mind find a better way to do something. Some people find it helpful to brainstorm on their own, while others aren't able to move their mind away from a certain focus in order to come up with action steps.

If this happens, it can be helpful to brainstorm with someone else who understands the end result that you want to achieve. Brainstorming with someone else is as simple as having a conversation.

You simply tell them what you want to accomplish and say that you're trying to come up with action steps that you need to take. Many times having someone else to bounce ideas off of can help you discover new ways to get things done that you may not have thought of on your own.

Brainstorming can also be helpful when it comes to seeking a solution about an action step. Some action steps require more effort than other ones do. You may end up needing to do more or find additional help.

If you don't have someone to connect with as a personal contact or even an online forum friend, you can start researching the best way to achieve certain goals online.

Be very specific when you search. For example, if you needed the mini goals to build a list, you might type in "steps to build a list" and see what pulls up. You might discover a blog post or infographic that details these steps:

Define your target audience Create an attractive opt in offer Sign up with an email system Set up the list responders Create a squeeze page

Promote your opt in offer

Maybe you didn't have one of those listed in your mini goals, but now that you've seen it online, you can add it. It's easy to forget all of the small steps involved in achieving a larger goal. You don't want to forget something important along the way, or feel caught off-guard if you realize it half-way through and need to completely reorganize your goals.

It shouldn't require much time to brainstorm – or research. If you're visiting other sites, just pop in quickly, scan the resource to see if you already have those steps on your list, and write down anything that might be missing.

Step 4 - Implement Changes

Once you've finished, it's time to take action. You will be putting into place the ideas that were generated from your brainstorming session. When you begin to implement change, you have to understand that it's normal to feel a sense of unease.

Most people are resistant to change. Just know that it's normal and don't let it stop your progress.

Create motivation as you start making changes. You have to be your own biggest fan when it comes to what you're doing. Celebrate all of your successes. It doesn't have to be expensive or huge – just recognize your efforts and reward your accomplishments.

The fact that you're working toward a goal and doing things to get you to the finish line is something that should be respected and admired. Sometimes, there's nobody there but you to enjoy your success.

Keep your vision. When you're implementing change, you don't want to lose sight of your goal. Understand the value of the changes that you're making. In other words, realize what will happen if these changes *don't* take place.

As you implement change, make sure that you monitor what happens as you make the change. Stay alert so you will be able to head off any negative situations or obstacles that arise from implementing your action steps.

There will be some obstacles that you can't foresee and that you can't head off. For those, you will want to try to get to the cause of the problem quickly. Understanding why there's a difficulty implementing a change can help you know how to get back on track.

You also want to keep in mind that while you're implementing change now, you will see some small benefits right away. However, seeing the end result of some of the other changes may take a while.

As you implement these changes, make sure that you're continually revising your goals because as these changes take place, your goals will also change. It's okay to adjust your goals along the way, too.

Sometimes, when you're on the path to something greater, and you're educating yourself, you discover fantastic new ways of doing things. This might mean changing a mini goal, or even altering your large goal completely.

One thing you shouldn't do is allow yourself to get distracted by too many good possibilities so that you're forever chasing a shiny new object and never follow through on the action steps you have mapped out to reach the milestones in your personal or professional life.

Mastering Relationships

Each relationship that you have in life - regardless of who that relationship is with - has the potential to go through several different stages. You may end up going through all of the stages or you may only go through the basic ones.

The level of stages that you go through will depend on the type of relationship that it is as well as the strength of the relationship. Mastering your ability to navigate relationships can be very beneficial for you in life.

Not only can you be more fulfilled at home with your personal relationships, but it makes succeeding in your professional life much easier. You will be an expert at networking, forming bonds with your target audience, interacting with clients easily, plus much more.

The First Meeting

At this stage, which is also sometimes called breaking the ice, initial contact or making someone's acquaintance, you're at the point where you simply meet the other person.

Most first impressions are formed at the first meeting. Sometimes during this stage, people will immediately connect to one another or they'll decide right away that they don't like each other.

Finding common ground is helpful when you're meeting someone for the first time. If you're going into a meeting with someone that you hope to develop a professional relationship with, do your homework first.

If you can discuss a shared love of something, it creates an instant connection. During this stage of a relationship, things are usually kept on the surface.

The topics that are discussed are usually trivial or common subjects such as the beautiful (or harsh) weather. There is a sharing of words, but not necessarily a meeting of the minds.

There are no strong bonds formed at this stage. It's at this point that people decide how much they want to get to know you. Though the phrase "you can't judge a book by its cover" is accurate, at this stage in a relationship, judgments do take place.

A bad first impression has the potential to set the course if you run into this person again. If there is a sexual attraction (in a personal relationship situation), this is referred to as an infatuation stage.

In this stage, wearing rose colored glasses can certainly apply. People see the good and can develop a tunnel vision where they don't notice any red flags because the attraction is so strong.

Everyone leaves a first meeting, whether in a personal or a professional relationship, with the decision made to be open to getting to know the person more or closed to it.

Be careful during a first meeting that you don't make snap judgments. That person could be the one that's suited to take your personal or professional life to the next level.

Try to understand that some people might be distracted or even shy at the first meeting. Try to put your best foot forward and get out of your comfort zone a bit.

The Bonding Stage

This is the second stage in a relationship and it's also known as the involvement stage or the growing stage. It's during this part of a relationship that ties begin to develop.

A person has decided that they like the other person well enough to get to know them. This is where new friendships begin, romantic relationships deepen and professional relationships begin a back and forth connection.

When you see this person, you will experience gladness or will look forward to meeting up with them if they offer to get together for coffee, drinks, or to talk about business.

This is the stage that's not yet strong enough to withstand any sudden harsh situations between the participants such as betrayal, lies or unprofessional behavior.

As the bonding stage continues, people decide that they can or can't trust the other person to become a little more relaxed. They may lose their formal approach if it's a professional relationship.

If it's a personal relationship, they will start to let down their guard and allow the other person to know more about them and their lives that they usually keep protected.

These can be deep, intimate things in some cases. If all goes well during the bonding stage, the people involved will enter into a more intimate relationship. For business relationships, this is the stage where discussions about going into business together or helping one another are often started.

A commitment to the relationship takes place and you officially see yourself as that person's friend, or business associate. If the relationship is romantic at this stage, the two people involved move toward creating a much deeper relationship.

They'll start talking on the phone for long periods of time. They'll connect back and forth on social media and make plans to meet up for dates or to hang out. This is the discovery stage where you start to find out how the other person grew up, what their favorite things are - or aren't.

When the bonding stage is going on, the people involved in the relationships, whether personal or professional, are often showing the best version of themselves.

Both individuals are putting a good foot forward because they want to impress each other - they want to be in the relationship on some level. This part of bonding can be called the honeymoon stage.

Everything seems perfect. The man or woman is everything that you've always dreamed he or she would be. You've found your best friend or you've found what seems like the perfect business partner or associate.

Life couldn't be going more your way. It's a beautiful thing and nothing that anyone says to you that has the potential to change the relationship or tear you apart from it sinks in.

You know there's no such thing as a perfect relationship - except this one - because you fit so well with this person romantically or professionally. While trust does develop in this stage and there is a back and forth of revealing a more personal side to the other, there's not 100% transparency in the relationship because wanting to impress the other person and gaining their favor is still the most important aspect.

You don't want to lose them or they don't want to lose you. Understand that in the bonding stage, you may not be seeing the real person. Unfortunately, there are those who wear masks so well, even they don't know who they truly are any more.

At this point, if you feel like something's off about the other person, trust your instincts and back off. You don't want to immerse yourself deeper in a bond that could potentially cause problems for you later.

The Discovery Stage

This stage can also be called the honeymoon's over stage. It's at this stage where all relationships get a big reality check. It's here where the disagreements and conflicts have the potential to show up.

In the bonding stage, you were more focused on building the relationship, on the excitement and newness of it all. But at this stage, you rediscover that you have an opinion and that it's sometimes different from the other person's opinion.

At this point, little issues can become big ones. You start to see that the person who could do no wrong - is actually wrong. You find out that the person you have a professional relationship with doesn't handle things the way that you would expect them to.

The rose colored glasses are thrown off and the faults of the other person can be seen clearly for the first time.

Some of these faults simply boil down to different life perspectives which do not mix well together.

But other faults can be cause for some major concern. For example, if you're in a relationship with a guy or girl who splurges on super expensive weekend getaways attempting to impress you, it may be that the person is simply foolish with money or just immature. And you know this type of behavior can cause serious financial problems down the road.

The professional relationship with the joint venture partner or client who trusted you to "handle this" is suddenly seen as a shift in the work relationship balance. You're doing all the work and they're taking all of the credit.

You might suddenly disagree on the direction that your joint business venture should take. Maybe assumptions were made on both sides, and it wasn't until this stage that you both realized you were split on the future.

This is the stage in a relationship where the work begins. You and the other person have to strive together for what will make the relationship successful. At

this point, you might feel a little like you've been betrayed because that person is not who you trusted that they were.

In a romantic relationship, this causes misunderstandings to develop. It can cause you to feel anxious, depressed or angry. You feel cheated out of what you thought was perfect.

This can be a stage in every relationship that can be used as a way to have open, honest communication about what's working for you and what's not. It can strengthen the relationship.

Or, it can lead to wounds that will continue to grow within you or in the other person and it lays the groundwork for the relationship to be over. With a professional relationship, once there's been a loss of trust, it has to be rebuilt or the union won't last.

This is the point where you have to decide if it's worth trying to salvage the relationship or not. In the discovery stage, be prepared that what you might find out could cost you emotionally or professionally.

If the initial bond was strong enough, you will have to make a decision whether or not it's worth it to patch things up and move forward in a new direction. If it's not worth the hassle, then finding out sooner rather than later will save you a lot of frustration.

The Conflict Stage

This stage is one that can also be referred to as the crisis stage. The relationship has reached a head. Major issues have been revealed. In a romantic relationship, this can sometimes be a series of thoughtless behaviors by a partner.

It can also be a loss of trust - such as is caused by an affair. The commitment that you made to one another goes through some serious unraveling.

The amount of stress that you will carry at this stage can be immense. You might feel pushed beyond your ability to care for the other person. Some people refer to certain types of conflict as deal breakers.

They know ahead of time what they will or will not put up with in a relationship. For some people, cheating is a deal breaker. For others, it's some type of an addiction - or the inability to give the relationship the proper care that it needs to thrive.

In a professional relationship, there can be issues that threaten the ability of the business to continue - such as poor management decisions. One partner isn't holding up his or her end of the deal.

At this point in either relationship, you will experience an internal struggle of whether or not to cut your losses.

You may start to think of the consequences of sticking with it versus leaving.

The conflict stage can continue on until communication is completely broken down. Instead of feeling excited about the once wonderful relationship, you resent the amount of time that you've spent attempting to make it work.

You feel like the relationship is all one sided. No amount of trying to talk over what's going on seems to be working. Maybe you've even spoken with a trusted third party and that hasn't made a difference.

You feel as if your boundaries have all been crossed and you feel a strong desire to get away from it all. You might feel like you have more peace in your life whenever your partner is busy with other things, away for awhile or when you're not interacting with him or her.

The relationship has reached the point that not only is communication absent but so is the presence of any physical or sexual intimacy, if the relationship is personal.

If it's a professional relationship, at this stage, with all of the conflict, you might feel like there's so much garbage between yourself and your business partner, that there's no way that it can successfully be dealt with.

The conflict stage can be a wake up call for any relationship. It can make people aware that there's a need for help if the relationship stands any chance of being salvaged.

But it's usually at this point where many people decide whether or not to enter the next stage of a relationship. With the conflict stage, make sure that you know ahead of time what you will do when disagreements arise.

This will help you to not say things you can't take back. It's always better to respond rather than to react. It can help if you study how to resolve conflicts - especially when it comes to professional relationships.

You don't want to jeopardize future partnerships by developing a reputation as a hot head. You want to be known for civil disagreements and pleasant parting of ways if the situation calls for it.

The Repair Stage

Sometimes, a relationship can be repaired. In this event, if it's a personal relationship, the people involved make a decision to do whatever it takes to salvage the relationship.

This usually involves a decision to change the actions that caused the relationship to break down in the first place. There's usually a commitment at this point to work together on resolving conflicts in a way that both partners can agree on.

You determine that you will be supportive of each other. You agree that you won't bring up the past, that you won't throw mistakes in the other person's face. You offer kindness to each other where harshness may have formerly been.

In a professional relationship, you may decide that it's worth saving because it's keeping you on track for where you want to be in the future. You might find it helpful to have an honest conversation in whatever professional relationship isn't working.

If you don't have a business or networking partner who is open to conflict resolution, you may have to expand your ability to not let the other person's actions get to you.

Sometimes, though, the relationship and the trust in it is simply too fragile to continue on. The repair stage can be a hard place to be in. You have to ask yourself if saving the relationship is worth it.

You need to know what it will mean to your life personally or professionally for your future if you let it go. Go through this stage with extreme caution. If necessary, make some concessions to the other person. Learn how to compromise to get past obstacles.

The Termination or Dissolution Stage

The erosion of trust in any relationship can lead to a termination or dissolution of the relationship. This is usually not a decision that's reached quickly by most people.

It happens over time when no compromises can be reached. The damage in the relationship is too great to be healed because the initial threads of the bond have unraveled to the point that no amount of talking can restart the relationship.

Many people choose to go in this direction in order to protect their emotional, financial or professional well being. If you reach the termination stage, don't look back.

Don't dwell on what you could have or should have done - on how you could have avoided what you went through. Harboring a lot of "what if" or "if only" thoughts will keep you tied to that relationship burden. Move on into the future with a forward focus on new beginnings and lessons learned.

Building Your Network

Networking is creating a foundation of connections that can boost your business, motivate and support you with all of your efforts. If you're an entrepreneur or business owner, the proper network will benefit you and your success greatly.

Having people surround you who can motivate and inspire you, as well as share knowledge that can catapult you to the forefront of your niche – is always a good idea.

You don't want all of your networking efforts to be in just one area (such as list building) - because that can narrow the positive benefits for yourself and the people you're connecting with.

You want to network with people who excel in a variety of ways so that you can learn from all of them and bring your business to a higher level. How you connect to these people should also vary.

You can connect with face-to-face encounters in your personal and professional life. You can make connections on social media sites, through email contact or on forums.

You can connect with a network both far and near by text, phone calls and webinars, too. The sea of networking is a vast, endless supply of connections just waiting to be tapped into by a go-getter like yourself.

Why You Need to Network

While being a solo entrepreneur sounds wonderful, it can also put a lot of pressure on you because you don't have a support system or team of individuals to help you succeed.

Networking can keep you moving forward with your goals. Though the term "self- made man" sounds great, in reality, no one person succeeded without a single bit of help through his or her lifetime.

Somewhere along the line, there was at least *one* person who reached out and helped them get where he or she wanted to be with a dream or a goal. By connecting with other people, there can be a source of help waiting for you that will provide you with encouragement and tools to continue moving forward.

When you move forward, obstacles often happen. Sometimes very often - and sometimes huge. When you have a network of people - it can help you find a path through or around anything trying to stop your success.

It might be that your sales copy isn't converting – or your product sales are low. Networking brings people into your life who can confidently speak up and help you pinpoint the issues and resolve them.

It helps because when you're striving for something in your personal or professional life, having a connection with people who have walked in your shoes helps to strengthen you.

When you're building a network, make sure that some of the people you connect with are heading the same direction. You want to do this because those people will be able to understand and they'll be able to "get you" – unlike those who aren't going after a similar goal.

But make sure you have a variety of contacts - because sometimes someone who is on a *different* path can offer a unique point of view for your vision and inject fresh ideas into an otherwise stagnant path.

By having a solid network, you will get the feeling that you're not in it alone. On the days that it can be difficult to keep on going, others are there to help you shoulder the burden or get your mindset to a better place.

This can also help create momentum when you feel like you're beginning to lag in motivation or enthusiasm. You need a network because you will find people that you can bounce new ideas off of.

You will also have others who can help you come up with new ideas. Or they may be able to suggest going in a different direction when the one you're on is filled with more obstacles than you anticipated.

In almost any endeavor in life, our emotions are closely mixed with whatever it is that we're doing. When you have a team of people you network with, you will often find a great network of emotional support.

You will be able to see that whatever happens - good or bad - in your life, doesn't have to change who you are. You will be able to look at how others handle success and how they deal with setbacks.

With a good network, you can create partnerships or joint ventures that can lead to even greater opportunities. You can double the amount of output you're capable of when you have a network.

You will also gain the benefit of others who may have more experience and wisdom with the project that you're dealing with. Maybe they know a shortcut or can help you avoid a disastrous result by offering a bit of advice.

Utilizing the Give and Take of Networking

When entrepreneurs think of networking, it's usually in a "What can they do for me" mindset. But the best way to get the top contacts in your corner is to step up and serve others *first*.

With networking, you have a great deal of ways that you can benefit. People that you network with also stand to gain from the relationship. This give and take of mutual benefits can help support your end goals.

With your professional colleagues, they can offer help with some of the projects that you need to do or some of the situations that you need handled. They can be a sympathetic ear when you need one and you can often find a group of people who will have your back when the time comes to stand up for something.

In exchange, you can offer help with projects they need help with as well as offering the same support when they're in need of someone to listen to them brainstorm or vent.

If you're trying to build a network with your clients, this can benefit you by giving you someone who will root for you, someone who can help you reach your professional goals such as an increased client list.

You can benefit this person by offering loyalty and the commitment to give each task your peak performance. Make sure you over-deliver and they will often reciprocate for you in the form of recommendations and bonuses.

You will want to build networks with assistants and others who work closely with people that you want to network with. These are the people that protect their bosses from just anyone being able to reach them.

They help streamline a busy person's day and keep them on target. By creating a strong network with assistants to the people you'd like to reach out to, you can create that chance for direct contact.

What you can give back is gratitude and support that shows you appreciate the effort. Assistants are often underappreciated and having someone acknowledge their work means more than you realize.

Network with people who know more than you in whatever area you need the help with. You will gain from their wisdom, their years of experience - and their contacts can become your potential contacts as well.

You can give them back fresh ideas, help with a project and be someone to bounce ideas off of. You can also help promote them and their products and services if you truly believe in the quality that they deliver.

Others who are also looking to network can be great connections to make. When you're networking with others looking to do the same, you can stay in the loop of what's going on in your field.

Fellow networkers can also be helpful at finding openings for project bids, for new opportunities, for sales and for potential career advancements. These people can help you be more aware of information that you need onhand in order to meet your goals.

They can share contacts and news for the field that you're in. You can then do the same for them. For instance, you might network with what is normally viewed as a competitor, where you each help the other build trust and loyalty with your audiences by co-hosting a webinar together.

You also want to network with community groups in order to create a platform, gain solidarity and share information with you. For their help, you can offer your expertise for their association or movement.

Networking with friends and family members offers good connection possibilities to help you reach your end goals. Family and friends can offer emotional support as well as be a sounding board and in exchange, you can do the same for them.

Go Where the Opportunities Exist

When you're looking to network, you do have to put yourself out there to make connections. Even if you're making connections online, you still have to reach out.

Regardless of where you plan to connect, make it a priority to try to create at least one new networking opportunity every day. It may take a few contacts to make a solid connection.

LinkedIn is a great place for connecting, but so are forums in your niche, Facebook groups, and even direct networking platforms like Twitter. All you have to do to find the opportunities is use the site's search function with keywords.

When you're trying to connect, don't overwhelm the person with eagerness. You can network without coming across as too pushy. Keep in mind that other successful people have busy schedules and they may not respond for longer than you think.

Look for organizations of similar interest. If you're into making and selling jewelry and you're hoping to network because your end goal is to grow your business, then you need to network with professional organizations and leaders in the same niche.

This might be an association for jewelry makers. The association might be one that breaks down the jewelry by the kind it is - such as contemporary jewelry. You would also want to look for stonesetting or stonecutting organizations.

Many of those will offer valuable resources that can link you to further networking opportunities. One thing you have to remember is that joining isn't enough – you have to be an active participant.

How are people in a group going to know who to recommend for you to network with if they're unaware of your position in the marketplace? So don't be afraid to be vocal about what you do and where you plan to take your business.

Look up trade organizations in the field that you're in. Pay attention to local and statewide organizations as well as national and international ones. These organizations can also help keep you in the loop on the latest trends and news in your area of interest.

You can get to know other people within these associations that form a bigger community and a greater chance of networking. Reach out to individual members who seem active and form closer bonds and friendships.

Go to as many conferences as you can possibly attend every year. You will be able to mingle with others who can offer you resources and connections to help you reach your end goals.

You will gain practical advice, be able to learn from someone else's knowledge - and come away feeling inspired. Plus, You will enjoy the company of like-minded individuals.

Make sure that you have an easy way that others at the gathering can contact you. You will want to have a flier or business card handy. These people will be meeting and interacting with so many others – and you don't want your name to get lost in the crowd.

If you have a book in print, then you might have a few onhand to pass out to special connections – and make sure you autograph it with a personalized message and your contact information, too.

Go online to find the networking opportunities that you need. Many of the organizations that you will seek have an online presence. You can easily engage and interact on a business's social media page or on their blog page.

If there's not something already online for a networking opportunity in the field that you're in or starting in, then create one. You can bet that if you're looking to network and nothing's available, that others are too - and they will find you.

Networking opportunities are abundant in many areas where you can find support both for your personal and professional goals. Being a part of a community should help you be more productive, so make sure you don't join one that seems to drag you down.

You Have Your Network - Now What?

After you've sought out networking and made those initial contacts, you want to make sure that you take the opportunities offered to you among this initial network.

But eventually, if your circle of networking remains the same and you're not adding new connections, you will lose momentum. It should always be growing at a steady rate.

Once you have your network in place, you can't let it stagnate. A network needs to be active for it to remain viable. There are several ways that you can cultivate your relationships in this network - and this will work for personal or professional goals.

Stay active. Too many people network to help reach their end goal and then they slack off. They join organizations and are so powered by motivation and determination at the beginning, but then they end up giving up. Why?

Because when they start accomplishing mini goals or reach the one big goal, they start to take it easy, believing they've arrived and no longer need anyone else's support to succeed.

Success is not an arrival. It is a continual pattern of growth. If you joined organizations to make networking connections, you need to keep up with those organizations on a regular basis.

Even if you don't have the same amount of time that you had in the beginning, you still need some kind of time commitment in order to keep the contacts you have interested and to build new ones in the future.

Participate in discussions within the group. Post insightful news and even share your accomplishments and compliment other people on theirs. Don't be gone from the group so long that you have to reintroduce yourself every time you stop back by.

People can tell when you're networking without reciprocating, so it's important that you give back. Whatever it took to build your success is what it will take to keep it growing.

It's a basic formula of lather, rinse, and repeat - only in the case of reaching goals, it's network, build, and repeat. Speak up about your accomplishments. Not in a bragging way, but in a way that's designed to create new networking opportunities that are borne out of someone being impressed by your momentum and accomplishments.

Spread your joy and passion for whatever you've accomplished. People love a good, motivating story.

You can be used to inspire others - and in turn, that will help create more networking contacts through word of mouth.

You can speak at schools, colleges, men's or women's groups - you can start podcasts or upload video presentations. All of these are forms of continuing to network.

When you need help with something, don't be afraid to speak up and ask for it. Likewise, when you see someone floundering, be the one who steps up and lends a helping hand.

Top 5 People You Want in Your Network

It won't do you any good to create a network if you build it with people who don't support your end goal. Having the wrong network can turn out to be worse than not having one at all.

There are five specific types of people you want to include in your network. These people will be instrumental in helping you achieve your goals.

The first person that you need to have alongside you is a mentor. This individual will be able to offer you guidance and advice. He or she can suggest when the time is right to take an opportunity - and when to wait.

They may also be able to help keep you from making a mistake. It's wise to have someone on your side who's been there, and done that. You can learn from their knowledge as well as from their setbacks.

A mentor is great at helping you build your self esteem to the point where you can rely on your gut instinct. They help with pinpointing your obstacles and the places where you feel most vulnerable, giving you the power to make good choices.

Opposite of a mentor, you also want to have someone that *you* mentor. This is because having someone in your network that *you* help along the way will work to keep your leadership skills increasing.

Someone that you're mentoring can help you with fresh ideas as well. You get to see where your niche needs help and find ways that will assist others in reaching their end goals, too.

In your network, you also want a creative thinker. Many creative thinkers are also dreamers. This will be someone who will cheer for your ideas and support your dreams - even if you haven't taken a single step to make those dreams a reality yet.

Creative thinkers are people who help you learn how to set yourself apart from the crowd in your niche. You have to be able to differentiate yourself within the niche if you want to keep achieving bigger and better goals along the way.

This type of person is someone who you can bounce ideas off of and then brainstorm an amazing result that will wow your audience and make your competition (and prospective JV partners) sit up and take notice.

But besides the creative thinker, you also want the analytical thinker. This person won't be someone telling you that something can't be achieved. Instead, he or she will be someone who can help keep you grounded.

Not all dreams and ambitions are meant to come to fruition. This person can help you see what steps you do need to take in order to have the success that you want. If something is unattainable, they'll not only tell you that it is, but why – so that you can find a workaround, if possible.

Finally, you need someone who's good at finding information for the purpose of helping you get ahead with your goals. This person will connect you to people or opportunities.

They will help find ways for you to network that you may not know about. This type of person loves introducing mutual friends who they know could use each others' ideas.

Building your network is an evergreen task that you should always be pursuing. You have to be able to simultaneously take risks in connecting with someone who might shock you in a good way – and cautious about partnering up with those who can derail your best efforts or make you look like you're aligned with the wrong people.

Productivity Through Obstacles

Building a business can be an exciting time in your life. It can also be one of the most stressful and frustrating times for you. Any time that you start to do something - to move forward - things will show up that stand in your way, threatening your success.

These conflicts can arise in many different areas - and they can affect the level of productivity that you have. Learn to recognize these obstacles and how you can successfully keep on track when they do appear.

The problems overlap between your personal and professional lives. For example, problems at work can cause hostility at home, and vice versa. You need to become a master at handling obstacles with ease.

Being Overwhelmed

There are what seem to be a million tasks to get done every day in a business. You have to keep up with the day-to-day tasks while trying to juggle the new things that pop up.

Trying to grow your business while maintaining what you already have can quickly become overwhelming. This is why you need to have a schedule for when tasks need to be completed.

You can't control when the unexpected happens, but by sticking to a schedule, you have a better chance at getting things done. If an obstacle arises that stops a days' worth of productivity, you need to map out a plan to double up on other days until you're back on schedule.

You need a task list. Every single thing that you have to accomplish each day for your business should be on this list. Whatever impacts your business the most should be at the top of this list.

By doing this, you can prioritize the tasks in order of importance. The first few tasks on your list should be whatever it is that you *have* to get done in order to keep the business functioning.

You have to keep the doors open or the site operational, keep the sales coming in and the payroll going out, while keeping the customers happy for positive feedback and steady growth.

Figure out what tasks you have to do that will profit or benefit your company today. If the task is something that will provide you with a profit in the same week, make that task a priority.

However, if it's something that won't make a difference immediately, you can put that off until a later date and time. Some business owners find it helpful to use one of the "year at a glance" calendars to keep track of the tasks that have to be done in the future for their business.

If you're dealing with feeling overwhelmed, then it's highly possible that you've taken on too much responsibility. In order to stay on track with productivity, you will need to find a way to delegate or outsource what can be passed on for someone else to do.

It can be easy in any business to take on too much. The shiny new object syndrome can make you feel a need to try something different in the hopes of improving your business.

Then before you know it, you have twenty different things going on that, instead of helping your business, is slowly grinding it to a halt. If any task manager or any organizational tool takes you longer to actually use it than the benefit it offers, get rid of it.

This could be contributing to the obstacle of being overwhelmed. Simplify anything you can to keep productivity moving along when you're struggling. That means if you spent money on a software tool that is too confusing to use and it has a steep learning curve, stop using it.

Chalk it up to a lesson learned. If you have to simplify things by turning to a spiral notebook and a pen or pencil, then do it – if you find that you make more progress that way.

Some business owners find it helpful to seek a mentor when they're feeling overwhelmed, while others turn to the services of a coach to help them clearly see their goals and how things are fitting into their lives.

One of the biggest issues in a business that can trigger being overwhelmed to the point that it slows productivity is clutter. If you have a cluttered office or a cluttered system online, it can make it difficult for you to find what you need when you need it.

Keep everything organized as you go along to prevent this from being an obstacle. Sometimes that means letting go of projects you once thought were viable, but never have time for.

The Obstacle of Time Management

Taking on too much at once can lead to a time crunch. So can procrastination. The problem in a lot of businesses is a lack of planning for every step of a project - especially if the project isn't due right away.

It can be too easy to think that you have plenty of time, so you do other projects first (or, if we're honest, waste time on social networking sites). Then before you know it, you're suddenly faced with this deadline or launch date - and you're not sure that you will have enough time to get it done.

Everything that you need to take care of in your business should have an action plan. You should know every area of your business that has a completion date. One of the easiest ways to blow your reputation is by being the person who can't get jobs completed when you say they'll get done.

A simple way around the obstacle of time management issues that slow your productivity is to make sure that each project you have going on has a detailed list of action steps.

You don't want to tackle a big project all at once. It can lead to you feeling overwhelmed. The best way to handle this is to break down the project into mini tasks.

Use a calendar or other means to divide the project up into chunks. If you have a project that you know is going to take three months to complete, then do a little bit of work on it each week.

This way, when the due date arrives, you can be finished up with plenty of time to have done the job thoroughly and professionally. Rushed jobs can often affect the quality of the finished product and you don't want to present work that's less than your best effort.

To help with time management obstacles, you can outsource some of the work. Take the work that someone else can do that's usually a big time drain for you and pass it on.

You can still get the work done, but free yourself up to do other tasks. If you're in the business of supplying information products and you handle everything from the writing to the graphics to the formatting, you can easily hire someone else to run this area of your business.

If you put out a lot of information products, it might be worth your money to hire someone who keeps up with making sure the product is completed the way that it should be.

This way, you remove several tasks from your own to-do list. That would include sourcing freelance ghostwriters and graphics providers, evaluating deliverables, and getting the end product launched with JV and affiliate partners.

Many businesses have entire areas that they outsource to someone else. For example, many ad agencies take on too many client projects. So they turn around and hire freelance copywriters to write the ads.

This saves them time and money and allows them to be more productive. Focus on the skills you excel at and enjoy most – and find others to take over the tasks you least enjoy.

Other businesses allow an outside phone service to take care of their incoming calls. This way, they can focus on running the business and still have good customer service.

You might hire a virtual assistant to handle your customer service issues online. It's all about freeing you up for the most important money-making and personally gratifying tasks.

Cash Flow Problems

This obstacle is one that hits a lot of business at some point during their operation. Having financial struggles can be detrimental to the business itself and it can affect morale negatively, too.

Cash flow problems can be caused by the current economy, poor money management, not enough marketing, too much overhead and a lack of customer response for the product that you're offering.

It can be difficult to want to keep on going when you're facing cash flow obstacles. But what you have to do at this point is to remember what your dream was in the beginning.

Don't lose focus during the hard times. So often, a business will go through a rough patch financially - only to turn around in the blink of an eye. Yet too many

business owners get so discouraged when the cash isn't flowing, that they slow productivity.

This slowed productivity then affects the overall business, which contributes to the cash flow problem. There are short-term and then there are long-term cash flow problems.

Short-term cash flow problems can creep up on you suddenly - and sometimes without warning. For example, you could have a big customer account that brings in thousands of dollars a month and suddenly, the customer notifies you that he won't be needing the services your company offers anymore.

So just like that, your profit is slashed. If the obstacle is a short-term cash flow, you can turn this around in a short amount of time by picking up some easy jobs that your company can do to bring in money.

The faster you can bring in the money, the quicker you will solve your cash flow problems. If you're used to making $300 an hour consulting for businesses, cut your price by a percentage.

You could bring in several smaller companies or individuals who couldn't afford your services at the higher rate. Running a special to give your business an injection of cash helps you survive during the next planning stage.

Long-term cash flow problems are a bigger obstacle to keep your productivity on track with. When you have this kind of financial issue, it can lead to a lack of supplies, not having enough to pay yourself or your employees and struggles to pay your typical overhead expenses.

Usually, long-term cash flow obstacles do indicate that your business is headed that way long before they become an issue. For example, you might notice that invoices aren't being paid on time.

If you allow other companies or individuals to pay you in arrears, several slow payers could hurt your business. If this is the case, then you would need to cut off the company having access to your services until the debt was settled.

Never risk your business's viability over someone else's lack of responsibility. Take care of the matter and if necessary, replace a slow or non paying client with someone who is reliable.

Every business will always have an area where there's a money drain. Go over every section carefully to see where you can cut costs. If necessary, have a mentor look over your day-to-day business operations and make suggestions.

If you're a start up business and cash flow is an obstacle because you don't have any at all, then barter what services you do have to get what you need. It's also a good idea to consider working on other cash-generating ideas like freelancing or an offline job if you need money to pursue your dreams.

Other Productivity Obstacles

Your friends and family can be your biggest supporters when you own a business. But they can also be huge obstacles. People who care about you can fail to understand and not respect your work schedule.

They can drop by to hang out at the office when you know you should be working. Or if your office is at home, they can interrupt you several times during the day.

When you have a business, setting boundaries to keep productivity flowing can be an issue. This is why you must set and keep clear-cut boundaries. You have to speak up whenever lines are crossed.

You must treat your business like a business and respect it - or others won't either. Sometimes people who work in a similar field will show up unexpectedly to talk, and this can temporarily slow you down.

Other times, they come by so often that it becomes an issue. If this is a problem, you will have to take control - and it can be as simple as saying, "I'd love to chat, but I have a deadline, so I have to get back to work."

Employees can create productivity problems when they don't do their job. When one person fails to do what he's supposed to do, it can have a trickle down effect. The project could slow down until someone goes back to complete the original task.

Mistakes are inevitable. Repeat mistakes and repeated issues of not completing assignments on time affect your business negatively, slow productivity will cost you in long-term profit.

If you have employees or an outsourced team that slows down your business, they either need retraining or to be replaced with ones willing to do their jobs correctly and on time.

Sometimes, it's vendors that can slow your productivity. They don't deliver a product when they're supposed to, so that can slow down the time a shipment needs to go out or a launch needs to take place.

You can work through this by finding a replacement vendor. If someone makes a commitment to have something to you by a certain day at a certain time, that commitment should be kept - otherwise, your business is the one most affected.

Sometimes, in an effort to save money and offer goodwill, business owners hire family members or friends. Working with people that mean a lot to you can be a great opportunity.

Loved ones and friends working toward a common goal can often increase productivity. But if you have a family member or a friend who doesn't do what they're supposed to, that can be a big problem.

In order to protect the family or friendship, you might not want to give that person the boot from the business but instead move them to an area where what they're doing won't impact the productivity.

If possible, let them the answer phones, handle email or do other tasks that help. But don't be afraid to put your foot down if there's nowhere else to put them. You're in charge of turning your business into a success, and you need to adhere to your own responsibilities.

Overcoming a Negative Mindset

How you feel impacts how your business runs. If you're experiencing something in your personal life, it can slow productivity. For example, if you're dealing with a family situation that causes you to lose sleep at night, it can be hard to keep your mind on the tasks at hand the next day at work.

If you have to deal with something out of the office that impacts your productivity, you need to take a step back and let someone else handle what you normally take care of in the business.

It can be a problem if you don't have a second in command who can run things for you. If that's the case, then you have to find a way to clear your head and push through.

One of the ways that you can do this is by assigning a specific time to think about and work on problems that occur outside of the office. You have to take care of yourself before you can take care of business.

Having the mindset that you've learned all there is to know can be a productivity obstacle. In this case, people will continue to do what they've always done - even if there's a better, faster, and less expensive way.

Not being teachable can easily cost you in terms of less productivity. Companies who produce tangible items or even strategies for you to learn from are counting on your ability to be open to growth through learning.

You will be doing yourself a disservice if you turn a blind eye to opportunities that can help you be more productive just because you're comfortable with the status quo.

Obstacles are a given in life. You have to strengthen your ability to handle them without panic. Once you learn the right way to navigate toward your goal, you will find that the once intimidating obstacles put in your path look much less frightening over time.

Success Mindset

It's clear that life doesn't divide up all good things evenly among all people. You can tell that just by people watching. Some people are better looking than others. Then there are people who are richer than their friends and family members.

There are people who come from a good background. They have a great education. They're intelligent, well-liked - and it appears the world is theirs for the taking.

Then, there are people who are average in looks. They don't have all of the money they need, much less all that they want. They come from backgrounds full of various struggles. They may not have attended a prestigious college - or even any college at all.

Yet, so many times, it's this second group of people who end up far more successful and enjoying more personal satisfaction than the first group. The reason for this is mindset.

Remember that someone who seems to have it all doesn't always stay that way. And what you see on the outside – the nice car, the fancy clothes – doesn't necessarily reflect inner happiness.

It's not enough to wake up every day and tell yourself positive things. That's a great start, but mindset isn't enough to change your life. You have to have an active role in taking action to leverage mindset into a new existence for you.

Understanding Mindset

It's not your past or current circumstances in life that determines what you can or can't achieve. Being successful in life is something that can happen for anyone because the key to success in business or in your personal life is having the right state of mind to carry you forward.

There are two kinds of mindsets. One of these appears successful - but in the end, that success will stall out. The other mindset will pave the way to a life full of personal accomplishments, business achievements and deep inner satisfaction.

The first mindset is called a fixed mindset. This is what people have who rely on what they know, what they're born with and what they believe they're capable of currently to succeed.

They believe that they have everything they need within themselves. This sounds positive, and in some ways – it is. But sometimes they run into obstacles and because they don't see anything they currently possess to handle it, they falter and fail.

But with people who have a growth mindset, they believe that anyone can work hard and achieve success. They don't have a quitter's attitude toward achieving success. This attitude causes them to continue to learn and take action while others coast by and get stopped by roadblocks.

The two differences can be compared to the race between the turtle and the rabbit. This was a race between unequals. If anyone were to bet on success between these two opponents, they would have bet on the rabbit.

From the outside, he had everything. He was faster - because his body and speed guaranteed that. Surely, he would finish the race with success because he started out equipped to win.

But as everyone knows, the story didn't end up like that. The turtle was the victor because he wasn't afraid to keep on going - despite the fact that the odds weren't in his favor.

He didn't have the speed or talent the rabbit had, but he was willing to stay in the race because he knew what the rabbit didn't. He knew that while he didn't have the ability to run very fast, he had the ability to go at his own pace and cross the finish line.

That race's outcome was determined by mindset. The rabbit also got complacent and didn't even try to create a strategy because he had assumed it was a given that he would win.

Your mindset has three parts that make it work - your IQ, the behavioral patterns you've learned, and your abilities. In those with a fixed mindset, they think that they have the talent and behavioral patterns they were given - and it's set in stone.

They believe this guarantees them success because of their talents. And if there ever happens to be something they can't do, they don't attempt to push through it because they don't believe they're capable of doing more than they currently can.

Though people with a fixed mindset can achieve some success - and many do - the level of success has a ceiling. The kind of massive success that they want always seems to elude them.

And it always will, because they keep on doing what they've always done - relying on themselves and foregoing any chance to grow so they'll know how to be the successful person they want to be.

But in people who have a growth mindset, it means that they're highly teachable. They're willing to learn what they don't know. They believe that they might have some natural ability or talent in an area, but that it needs to be cultivated.

They realize that they can always improve on what they already know. They're not afraid to try and fail because they understand it's a common part of learning and achieving.

People with growth mindsets are willing to put forth whatever effort is needed to achieve success. They're willing to take continuous action that will move them toward their goals and their dreams.

Look back on the past three months of your life. Think about whether you've had limited self talk which convinces you that you can't go after something "out of your league".

Have you quit on a project or partnership because you felt it was simply too much for you to handle? That's a sign that your actions aren't aligned with the positive mindset you've adopted over time.

Letting Go of the Wrong Mindset

If you have a fixed mindset, it doesn't mean that you're stuck with it. Being aware is half the battle. Your mindset is something that can be changed - depending on how you cultivate it.

First, you have to be able to identify the mindset that you have. You need to understand that your mindset can be fixed with one issue, yet be leaning toward growth on other issues.

This occurs because though there are two definable types of mindsets, you can have times where you cross the line from one to the other - and your mindset becomes a mixture of the two.

You can tell if this is what you're experiencing by your inner thought patterns. If you feed yourself limited thoughts, then you're in a fixed mindset. Fixed mindsets will often first focus on the negatives in any situation before they see the potential.

Fixed mindsets will close doors to opportunities while growth mindsets seek ways to open them. An example of being in a fixed mindset would be inner thoughts like, "You don't have the right talents for this. You're not intelligent enough. You will make a fool of yourself if you try."

These fixed mindset thoughts keep many people from trying new ideas or venturing out on their own. If you're not sure what pattern you're in, keep a journal of your honest feelings to gauge where your head is at over the course of a 6-week period.

A fixed mindset can keep people stuck in a routine, such as giving them the fear of leaving a job they don't enjoy - when they really want to start their own business.

If people with a fixed mindset decide that they're going to make a change and reach for an opportunity only to have it end badly, they'll hear a round of "I told you so" thoughts.

This leads them to believe that they're not enough - that they're better off not trying again. A fixed mindset can keep you trapped and prevent you from developing a strong success mindset unless you decide that you've had enough.

To change a fixed mindset to a growth mindset, you have to stop the negative messages that a fixed mindset feeds you. Instead of allowing yourself to believe thoughts like, "I knew I was a failure. I blew it." you would switch that to something like, "I know I'll find a way to succeed. Look at all of the setbacks others have had - yet, they made it and I can, too."

Understanding mindset so that you can let go of the wrong kind is one thing, but you have to know how to take action to support the other kind of mindset as well.

A Success Mindset Requires Action

Inaction is idleness. It means that you're not moving forward in any aspect of your life. You know you need to make some changes and know you want to put them into action, but you never actually do anything about it.

A success mindset can be harder for those who struggle with self-esteem. Maybe you had someone who told you that you couldn't do something that you always wanted to do.

Maybe you don't have a strong support system in your life. Or maybe you're the enemy of your own success.

That's what you are if you tell yourself that you can only accomplish so much and you shy away from your bigger goals and dreams.

You believe those are for others. The reason that you may believe others deserve it more than you is because you've convinced yourself that they're more talented, more connected, or even smarter.

Or you might have the right self talk, the positive mindset, but fear paralyzes you into procrastinating on the actual action of making beneficial life changes. You have to plan for your successful outcome.

Begin what it is that you want to do - even if every move you make is screaming that it's not going to end well. You want to do this because when you take action, your beliefs follow.

This is what trips up too many people. They think they must believe something before they take action, when it's the opposite. Take action, then watch how much you will believe in what you can accomplish.

Every time you complete a task toward your goal, you gain self confidence in your abilities. This is how you develop a strong success mindset. It's like working a muscle.

Action strengthens the belief. People who have a fixed mindset will often avoid taking action. They want to do what they know is safe - what they're already good at.

Because if they take an action step and it doesn't work out, it will make them feel as if they've failed. This is a hard thing for people with a fixed mindset to experience.

Some will never take that leap of faith again, while others will keep going because they want it so bad. It's action that takes someone with a fixed mindset and frees them up to the potential that is inside of them.

Using Your Mindset

Too many people make sweeping statements about what they want their success to look like. They follow this by coming up with goals that are vague and out of their control.

For example, if someone were to say, "I want to make a million dollars." that goal, while a lot of people have, is too broad. You can't take action if the success you want is too generic.

Making a million dollars would need to be defined by how, when, and what actions you need to take to reach that goal. If you were to say, "I want to make a million dollars on the stock market." then that gives your action a way to focus on the process.

You need your actions to be definable in order to develop a strong mindset that takes progress toward success. You would focus making your million dollars by learning all that you could about the stock market.

You would study tutorials, read books, and maybe even take classes. You would try to find a mentor. Each of these steps moves you toward what you've defined as your ultimate goal.

You would analyze where you are right now in your life so that you could clearly define the action steps needed. If you want to earn a law degree, but you didn't finish college, you would define one of your action steps as finishing college before you could apply to law school.

What helps when defining action is not to look down the road at where you're going to arrive some day, but to stay focused on the here and now. By being in the present, it's easier to continue taking action.

Like the turtle in the race, you focus only on the step directly ahead of you. You don't focus on how many more weeks or months or years it's going to take you to reach the success that you've defined.

The reason that you don't want to focus on the broader single goal is because that can lead to a fixed negative mindset. You're in a constant state of failure until that goal is reached.

If you're achieving mini goals on a regular basis, then suddenly the world is wide open to you because you have a growth mindset – you can see evidence of your consistent accomplishments and it reinforces your belief in yourself.

7 Habits That Lead to a Strong Success Mindset

To get what you want, whether it's in your personal or professional life, you have to learn to do what works. For most people, this means creating a habit. But a habit isn't something that never changes.

A success habit is always changing.

Habit #1 - Make sure what you want is really what you want.

Don't do something just because you *should*. Check in with yourself every 30 days to make sure that the path you're on is the one you want to stay on. Doing this prevents you from ending up with business models that don't satisfy you.

Make sure you're not abandoning something out of fear of failure. There's a big difference between doing what's right for you and doing something that feels easier.

Habit #2 - Begin every day with motivation.

These are things that work to get you to take the next step. For example, if you need to go for a run to clear your head and get some time to think, then do it. If you need to use specific habits every morning in order to get into the flow, then make sure to start each day with those habits.

Starting off with motivational reminders is like eating the proper foods – it helps to fuel you throughout the day. You also want to spend a minute or two looking back over your day and being proud of what you did accomplish.

Habit #3 - Don't chase success to the point that you stop dreaming.

Your success begins with an idea, a hope - a dream. If you go all out, driving hard, keeping your nose to the grindstone, you can reach the point where your mindset becomes fixed on the negatives.

All you can see is the end result rather than the journey. Try to remember on your way to getting what you want, that success is a journey and not a destination. You will never have these days, weeks, and months to live over again.

Sometimes it becomes a chore to just blast through a task list – especially if you forget about why you're doing everything. If your goal is to live on the beach in a nice home, make sure you routinely revisit those plans to keep you inspired with your action taking.

Habit #4 - Make sure you leave room to grow.

You need to have a success mindset that keeps you learning even when you feel you've made it. There's always something else that you can learn. Seek out new

resources online, books and new contacts who teach things from a different perspective – anything that helps expand your education.

Habit #5 - Answer to someone else.

You want to have someone in your life that you're accountable to. Make time to meet with someone who can help keep you on track for reaching your success. You want this person to be someone who can tell you when you're driving yourself too hard and someone who can help you avoid the pitfalls.

Sometimes you won't have a specific person in your life capable of doing that. You can turn to a paid life coach or even join a forum of like-minded, positive individuals all striving for their own success.

Habit #6 - Learn to trust yourself.

When you go after what you want in life, there will always be someone waiting to tell you that something is either a good idea or a bad idea. Everyone has a built-in alarm that will sound if something is off.

You will feel it as knots in the pit of your stomach or as a sense of unease. When you begin trusting yourself in these situations, it helps you develop a sense of self-confidence and strength.

Habit #7 - Understand that roadblocks are going to happen.

You have to determine ahead of time that you won't give up - you won't surrender a positive growth mindset to a fixed negative one. Roadblocks can often be used as character builders.

They can strengthen your resolve and help you learn to become more resourceful as you find another way to achieve what you want to get accomplished. If you become too comfortable with your efforts, you often don't achieve the ultimate success that you're after.

Having a strong mindset in life, whether for your personal or professional satisfaction, requires a combination of positive thoughts and verifiable action steps.

Whenever you do something that you start to feel a bit of shame over (like quitting on a project), ask yourself if you're doing it because you don't believe enough in yourself to succeed.

If that ends up being the case, take the task and break it up into micro-sized mini goals that you can work on to see if you're capable of making progress. Sometimes, it's the simple fact that a project appears too big that ruins many of the best plans.

It's also a good idea to surround yourself with action-taking, positive people. Take inventory of the kinds of people you're currently surrounded with. Do they always complain about everything?

Do you find yourself complaining with people stuck in the same boat as you? If so, jump out and swim to shore – because that boat is sinking fast, and you don't want to be swallowed up by the pity party they're throwing for themselves.

Seek out motivational experts whose thoughts align with what you find inspiring. Tune in to their messages or read their books daily as if you're taking vitamins designed to prevent illness.

Over time, you're going to become someone who others look to for support, and you will notice they come to you with fixed negative mindsets. They'll be attracted to the positive mindset that you project. Make sure you turn their mind around, and be very careful not to let their negative thoughts infect you.

Self Esteem Leeches

Having a healthy self-esteem means that you have confidence. You feel sure in what you can do. You like who you are as a person and you respect yourself. It means that you can see the value of being you.

Self-esteem is important because how you view yourself guides what you believe and how you feel. It can also impact how others feel about you. Unfortunately, there are leeches that can latch onto your self-esteem and drain it dry.

You want to protect yourself against these kinds of people, and sometimes, that means making the difficult decision to distance yourself from people who are close to you.

The Negative Leech

This is a leech that can be found in conversations. You can recognize it because this leech will try to make you feel bad about yourself. The words sound okay, but are said in such a way that they erode how you feel about yourself.

An example of a conversation leech would be, "Your dress is beautiful, but it would look better on you if you'd lose a few pounds." This is the sucker punch conversation.

The first part of it was kind and so you were relaxed and open. The blow came next - and many people are caught off guard. It affects the self-esteem because we tend to play this type of negative comment over and over in our mind.

You can get rid of leeches like this by responding with something similar to, "That's not very nice. Why would you say something like that?" A leech can only walk away with your self-esteem if you allow it to happen.

People who tell you that you're ugly or fat, stupid or worthless are self-esteem leeches. Don't give them another second of your time. Don't put up with these types of comments or people.

You are not their beliefs. Those statements are usually a reflection of them, not you. But what's worse than those kinds of negative leeches is when we become our own negative leech.

If we tell ourselves that we're ugly or fat, stupid or worthless we erode our own self-esteem. No one is born with this kind of self-talk. We learn it from a self-esteem leech.

Once you adopt their behaviors and you start saying this kind of stuff in your head, you'll find your quality of life rapidly declining.

The Social Media Leech

This has become a huge leech and it's growing bigger and draining the self- esteem from millions of people. Social media opened the door for so many people to become leeches.

They bully and they tear down others, they drain away at the self-esteem of others in order to build themselves up. They say nasty comments to people that sting way down deep.

Most people take the comments of perfect strangers to heart and don't take the time to recognize the comments for what they really are - the attitude and actions from someone who doesn't have the capacity for online maturity.

You have to ignore comments that try to tear you down on your social media sites. There are many people who consider themselves expert trolls – whose sole purpose is to cause friction online. It's their form of entertainment.

Social media can be a self-esteem leach if it causes you to look at someone else's life and be envious. What you need to remember is that social media usually presents a false perception of someone's life to the world.

You only get a peek at it. The perfect house, the perfect family, the smiles and laughter along with heavily edited photos don't show the true picture. Don't let these false representations tear down your self-esteem.

A lot of social media is embellished because people find it easier to present a better version of their lives online - and it often greatly differs from reality. Keep in mind that many people are too self-conscious to speak up about the sad side of their lives.

The Mistake Leech

You wouldn't be human if you didn't make mistakes. Some people make a lot of little mistakes, while others make mistakes that are pretty big. But you must realize the mistakes that you've made do not define who you are.

They're not a picture of your future. Mistakes are simply something that happened which can offer you the opportunity to learn from the situation and grow. The leech presents itself in this area by not allowing you to move on.

When we make mistakes, it's often those closest to us who won't let it go. They remind you of your mistake and it can feel like they're rubbing it in your face. They remind you how you tried to start a business and failed, how you ruined your finances, how they warned you that the guy or girl you were crazy about was bad news.

These mistake leeches can be hard to take, but even more so when you're the one putting the mistake leech on yourself. You continuously remind yourself about how you failed.

How you wish you hadn't done what you did. Get rid of this self-esteem leech once and for all by telling yourself that it's over and you've moved on in the right direction.

Tell others the same thing if they keep bringing it up. Don't drag your mistakes around with you and don't let others pile them on you, either. Take a firm stance against having the past thrown in your face to knock you down as you continue to better your life.

The Approval Seeker Leech

Some people have a laid back personality. Others have a more forceful personality. Both can have strengths to offer. But the problem arises when someone with a stronger personality decides what your life should or shouldn't be.

They try to make it so that you have to seek their approval in every aspect of your life. When you try to do something on your own, they're quick to tell you why that won't work and how it's not smart of you to attempt it.

What this does is erode your self-esteem until you're driven to come to them for advice and help with whatever you want to do in life. These kinds of leeches keep you dependent on them for your happiness (and theirs) and you surrender control of your life to them in return.

You don't need approval to be who you are and to live the kind of life you've always wanted. Your actions are your own and you're smart enough to reach for your dreams without having to seek approval.

If you don't know the way that you should go, take a deep breath and relax. You can learn. You are capable. You don't need anyone else's stamp of approval for your chosen path.

The Comparison Leech

This nasty leech is one that we put on ourselves and we all have trouble with this one. It can erode self-esteem pretty quickly and leave you feeling unhappy with your life - even if you have a pretty good one.

This leech makes you feel like you're not doing a good enough job with handling your life because it fails to measure up to someone else's. Even a multi millionaire can suffer from this as he compares himself to a multi billionaire.

The comparison leech piles on us when we feel envious of someone else. We can experience envy because they appear to have a partner or spouse who treats them better.

We can feel envious because their house is nicer. Their car is newer. Their clothes are more expensive. Maybe they have a better job. Perhaps they can afford to do home renovations that you wish you could do.

They get to take lavish vacations to places that you've dreamed of going. This kind of comparison robs you of living your life. You don't know what's going on in someone else's life and looking at it from the outside can often give you a distorted view.

It could be that you have more freedom than they do. That you're not in debt like they are, that you're not dealing with the emotional situations they're hiding from the world. You never know what's truly going on with someone else.

Get rid of this leech by recognizing and being grateful for the good that you have in your own life. Refuse to allow negative feelings to bother you over someone else's seemingly good fortune.

The What Others Think of You Leech

This leech steals self-esteem. We assume that people are thinking thoughts about us that are less than kind. We believe that they're having conversations and our names are being mentioned.

In these conversations, nothing good is being said. They're surely discussing the way that we look. They're talking about how poor our products are. They're discussing rumors they've heard about us.

Believing this makes us feel self-conscious and awkward. It robs us of what could be beautiful friendships and new opportunities because we shy away from these people or we keep them at arm's length - afraid to say or do something that will give them more fuel to think about us or talk about us negatively.

You can get rid of this leech by realizing that other people really aren't dwelling on you or your life. Most everyone is far too busy to keep up with someone else's life. They have all they can handle with their own situations.

So don't let yourself dwell on what you think others are saying. Worst-case scenario, you're right – they are ridiculing you. So what? Other peoples' opinions have no place in your life.

The Perfectionism Leech

This is the leech that will not allow you room to truly live. When you allow this leech to attach to your life, you don't leave room for much good because what happens is this leech brings with it the waiting game.

You have to wait until everything is perfect for you to make that move personally or professionally. You don't take chances with new ideas or ventures because perfectionism doesn't welcome mistakes.

You can begin to develop an all or nothing mentality. Perfectionism is a terrible leech because it can leave you feeling bruised inwardly. You will beat yourself up every time you make a mistake.

And since you *will* make mistakes as long as you're breathing, you will go through life thinking that you will never be able to do anything right. The perfectionism leech will convince you that you will never be good enough.

You will walk around believing that you're a failure before you even attempt to do anything. This leech keeps many people stuck in a life of wanting more but never reaching it because they would have to risk failure.

The Drama Leech

These are leeches that take from you, destroy your self-esteem and make you absolutely miserable. Many people are familiar with these leeches in their personal life.

They understand that people who take and never give back aren't good for them. With a drama leech, whatever is going on in their life is absolutely the most important thing - and you must help them deal with it immediately.

You have to put your personal or professional life on hold in order to comfort them, and keep them from going under. If you do this, you will get sucked in every time they need you.

This destroys your self-esteem when it reaches the point to where you can't be there every time they need you because it's impacting your life negatively. Your significant other isn't happy about the amount of time the drama takes you away.

You miss work or you can't concentrate on work because the drama leech is wrecking your time or taking over your thoughts. Your boss tells you that you're just not cutting it at work any more, or a business partner feels let down by your lack of focus and commitment.

To deal with this leech, you have to understand that for some people, drama is a lifestyle. While it may be true that they have problems, even a ton of problems, if you're always the one that rescues them, you've entered into a co-dependent relationship.

This drama usually comes from toxic friends or family – but it can also be people in your professional life - and if you don't rush in to rescue them, they turn on you.

They'll say that you're not doing enough to help them. You're not loaning them money, holding their hand, rushing over every time they call. They will give you nasty labels or tear you down.

You don't have enough empathy. You're mean. You don't love them enough. How can you be so selfish? When they say negative things about you, you can begin to believe the problem is you.

Especially if you're dealing with several family members or professional acquaintances in a group who are drama leeches, it can be a big drain on you emotionally and physically.

When you're always putting out fires for others and you realize someone is leaning on you too much, put your foot down and become unavailable so that they're forced to handle things themselves – or find someone else to turn to instead of you.

Yes, they'll be frustrated with you. They may even lash out, but that's because they're not comfortable handling their own obstacles. You don't want to enable them anymore.

The Disempowerment Leech

When your self-esteem is strong, you can speak boldly and with confidence about who you are and what you do or want from life. Disempowerment happens when others don't value what you do or what you want.

For example, for the person who wants to go to an Ivy League college, for someone else to say, "Oh they let anyone in there now" devalues your hard work and effort.

It steals your sense of accomplishment and pride. But you can also put this leech on yourself. For example, if you've always wanted to run an online crafts business and someone asks you what you do, if you downplay it, that can begin to lower your self esteem.

Don't downplay your accomplishments or make light of your hard work. The problem that this leech causes with your self-esteem is that it can affect your perspective.

You can recognize if you're disempowering yourself by how you speak about yourself or your life. If you say, "I wish I could start my own business," this is a disempowering way of thinking. Instead, change that to "I am starting my own business."

The Conforming Leech

This is the leech that looks at how things have been done and doesn't see a way to do it any differently. Its strength is found in tradition, in the way that things have always been done instead of the way that things can be done better.

This leech erodes your self-esteem by insinuating that your ideas are foolish and that there's no way they will work because no one else has ever been able to accomplish it.

You can talk yourself out of trying anything if you allow the conforming leech to dictate what you do or don't do in life. You might hear this referred to as the road not traveled.

The reason the road isn't taken and new ventures sometimes don't get off the ground is because people are afraid to stand out - afraid to run with an idea that others say can't be done or is different from the norm.

When you have an idea and you tell yourself that it's foolish or you allow others to convince you that it's foolish, your self-esteem takes a hit because you can start to believe that you're not as smart as others who have found success.

Start believing in innovation again. That's how life changes for the better. Stop putting limitations on yourself and free yourself from all of the chains that bind you physically, mentally, and financially.

Systematize Your Business

Being a hands-on entrepreneur is thrilling (if not quite overwhelming) at first. As you get your business off the ground, you become used to doing everything yourself.

Even when you start outsourcing to freelance individuals, you sometimes keep a tight leash on them to the point that you're continuing to waste valuable time you could spend elsewhere.

When you're too directly involved with the microscopic tasks of your business as it grows, your growth slows to a halt. Plus, you're unable to free yourself from the day-to-day operations of the company, which means no sick time, no vacations – and no reward for your efforts!

As you grow your business, there will be tasks that it no longer pays for you to do yourself. You will end up losing money by trying to handle everything on your own. There is a great way to continually build a business if you systematize as much of it as you can.

Gain from Systematizing Your Business

It might cost you some money up front when you set your system in place. But you end up gaining a lot more than you spend. Implement the systematized process as early on as possible, so that you're free to work on more profitable areas of your business.

The responsibility of making sure that the entire business runs smoothly is taken off your shoulders with systemization. Rather than losing money, a system can actually help keep your expenses lower and more manageable.

This will make a difference in your end result financially. One way that a lot of businesses lose money is by having overly capable people doing tasks that someone else can do at a lower cost.

For example, if you have a guy who makes $25 an hour do a task that someone else could do for $15 an hour, you will have lost $10 per hour for every hour the higher paid person works on the task.

If you're the one that's handling a task that someone else could easily do, then you're losing profit by being hands-on in that area. You want results with your

business, but you should find the cheapest, most efficient way to accomplish these results.

How do you know if you should systematize your business? That's easy. Ask yourself this question. Am I feeling overwhelmed with simple tasks that take me away from more important areas?

If the answer is yes, then it's time to start analyzing the automation potential your company has – as well as seeing what can be outsourced to other professionals. Don't look at it as, "I don't want to pay someone to do something I can do myself."

Instead, think of it like, "I'll pay someone to do this because I know I can increase profits if I'm freed up to focus on marketing and product creation." Is the cost of what you're outsourcing going to be worth the return you get? If not, then it might be something that should remain in-house.

How to Decide If You Should Systematize Your Business

Every area of your business has the potential to be systematized, depending on what the tasks are. The more often you do a task in your business, the greater the need for systemization.

Can you imagine a popular chip company that filled each bag of chips by hand? No conveyor belts, no machines to seal the bags or move them off the belt. The cost of running the business would skyrocket. You'd have to double the amount of manpower you had on the floor.

Take a look around your business to see what areas have a lot of tasks that have to be completed every day. These are usually some pretty mundane things that don't require a lot of thinking.

For example, you might have a high volume of people who need help downloading the product they just bought. That's a task that can be outsourced to a virtual assistant.

Or you might think of the time you'd need to spend learning how to set up an affiliate system and decide that paying the company to do it for you is worth it, since you could be focused on other money making projects while that's being done.

By systematizing, you give yourself back time and money. Your business will tend to have fewer glitches during operation and you can improve the way that your business interacts with people.

Maybe you manually deliver every product to your customers online. Using a shopping cart systematizes your business, automatically delivering download links, capturing the customer's name and email address, and adding them to your email autoresponder.

If you systematize, you can relax knowing that you don't have to be there every single second of the day to ensure that everything is being done properly. Sometimes, business owners decide to systematize based on the complexity of the task versus how often it needs to be done.

Systems are a means of taking your place when you're not there or are otherwise busy. Most business owners don't realize that systematizing does more than free up time and make things run more efficiently.

It also makes your business more valuable. Think about it. If you have to be there in order for it to run, that means that once you need to do anything outside of work, everything will grind to a halt.

The business will become worthless if it's not functional. You want to set it up in a way so that you can walk out the door, take some time off - and everything can run as usual.

Another reason to systematize is if you're starting to notice that you're letting your customers down. If you can't handle the influx of customer service emails, then do your customers a favor and outsource it to a ticket system or a virtual assistant who can prioritize and handle that for you.

Once you've made the decision to systematize, you will want to decide which particular parts of your business you're going to do that with. Some business owners choose to systematize only small portions while others choose to systematize anything that they possibly can.

Deciding whether or not this is right for you will depend on the system that you choose. Some of the systems are fairly simple and easy to implement. The simpler the system is, the less costly it will be.

However, you might be better off paying more for a high grade system - even if it costs more - because usually the more the system costs, the more benefits it offers a company to use it.

The System You Currently Use

There are a lot of businesses that do things a certain way because it's been handed down from generation to generation. Nothing has changed or updated in the many years of doing business - even if it takes more time and effort.

Then there are businesses that had to start on a shoestring budget, so they had to keep the costs to a bare minimum. The owner had to devise a system that could work on the limited budget that was available.

Here's the good news. Some of those limited budget plans and ways of running your business are good just the way they are. If something is working for you and getting the job done while still producing good client satisfaction, then you don't have to make any changes just for the sake of change.

Remember that systematizing a business is always done for a purpose. Some of these reasons could be for improving operations, offering better customer service, making an increased profit, following new guidelines and creating more productivity.

If what you have can't be sufficiently improved on in any of those areas, then you should leave it alone. Take some time and pay attention to how each of your systems operate.

Write down how each area of your business performs and how it's possible that it might be better handled. For example, if you have a business with hundreds of incoming emails every day, but only one person responding to them, you can bet that your business can improve its customer service if you add a more efficient system.

Once you have an overall picture of how your systems are operating, you will be able to see which ones could be changed to make your business more efficient. Even if you can't make all of the changes that you'd like to make at once, start by making the changes that you can.

Choose which area of your business should be systematized first based on the burden it's causing or the profit potential it has, and go with that one. Establishing a system that works right for your business might involve some trial and error - but the improvements will be worth it in the long run.

The Main Parts of Your Business to Focus Systemization On

Ordering and inventory is a good place to check for potential automation. If you have tangible products, then you will be handling orders as well as inventory at some point.

This can take a lot of time - unless you have automated delivery systems in place and automated inventory checkers. This allows your computer systems to do the time consuming tasks that can really add to your hours.

You save money by having a system that can handle anything you need to keep in stock. When you make a sale, you need to make sure that your business is systematized.

For example, if you have an online business and you sell information products, every time you make a sale, you have to send it out. If you're only selling one or two of these a day, then it's not a big deal.

But as your business grows, you could get hundreds of orders every day. To take the time to manually send out each order would not only keep you chained to your computer, but it wouldn't be a very efficient way of doing business.

Plus, you have to take into account how the customer feels. If you don't answer the order for a digital product for 2-3 hours, your customer will feel frustrated that you do not have an automated system in place to send them the product instantly and may not purchase from you again.

Handling the money is another area of automation to consider. By systematizing your business, you can set it up so that when a customer orders, the system takes the payment and sends the product immediately after payment is verified.

This frees you up to continue to make other items or to work on different tasks. You need to have a way to keep track of all kinds of payment options. You need to know what amounts come in and what amounts go out.

If you can't find the record of someone who says they bought your product, but now they want a refund, you could lose money by being forced to trust that customer's word if they don't have proof of purchase. Or you could risk damaging your business reputation by refusing to refund them for the item.

When you systematize, every order is documented, as are the refunds. Having a system in place can keep up with payroll, with the deposits you make for the

company, petty cash and with the company expenses that you have to pay and more.

Keeping up with invoices and making sure that your employees are paid correctly falls under a system that handles the money. So you want to make sure that whatever you use for that is systematized.

Customer service is an area that you really do need to make sure you systematize. Without happy customers, your business will suffer. You want to make sure that from the moment a customer contacts your company, they experience a convenient and easy way to get their needs met.

This can happen if you have a ticket system that alerts you to high priority situations, or a virtual assistant who handles incoming customer communication as it occurs.

With systemization, you can have a cordial, professional greeting that your customers receive on autopilot, letting them know you received their inquiry.

You always want to make sure that you're continuing to generate interest and income for your business. This means that you have to keep those leads coming in for future profits.

You can't do that unless you're reaching out. If you're trying to do everything yourself or you're having others do it manually, you could miss out on reaching more potential customers.

You have to bring in customers to keep your business thriving. By systematizing the lead generation process, you can be acquiring new business while you work on other things.

Even when your business is closed for the day, and you've taken off to recover from an illness or to have a day out with your family, a systematized tool such as an autoresponder opt in form paired with an online ad campaign can let your business keep working automatically for you.

You can systematize in other areas of how you brand yourself and connect to your audience, too. There are tools that help you schedule content, run ads, and launch new deals to your customers – without you having to be there helping it all unfold.

Implementing the System

Change can be a difficult thing for people to embrace. Whether it's you struggling with the new and improved system, or your customers having to get used to a new way of interacting with you, be aware that there may be an adjustment period.

Make sure that when you systematize your business, you let your audience know how it works. Take the time to explain the changes and why it will be beneficial for everyone if it's done this way.

When you set up or arrange to have your system in place, pick a day of the week and a season that you're not scrambling to complete a project. You don't want to add any unnecessary stress if you can help it.

Everyone who needs to use the system needs to understand how to operate it. Confusion can cause a lot of setbacks and you don't want that. It might take you or your outsourcers a few days or weeks to get the hang of a new system.

Allow time for this. Don't implement something the day before a brand new launch – where you and your customers will experience a lot of frustration if there are glitches or confusion happening.

Once your system is set up and operational, you will want to do periodic spot checks to make sure that it's working the way that you want it to work. If it's causing more time and hassle because it's too complicated, then obviously, the system isn't working for you.

Systematizing a business is intended to make life easier for you as you run your company. If it doesn't do that, then it needs to be tweaked or changed. Sometimes there is a simple fix, and other times, you have to chalk it up to a loss and find a replacement.

The goal with systematizing your business is ultimately increased profits. Every change you make, you should analyze the return you expect to get from the new way of doing things.

For instance, if you hire a virtual assistant part time and pay her $20,000 a year, then you should expect to see your profits shoot up more than $20,000 per year because she's now handling the drudge work and you're able to focus on money making efforts.

Sometimes, an entire area of your business can't be automated. But a portion of it can. You need to map out the entire process of each area of your business and see if there's anything you can plug in to automate a portion of that task.

For example, with blogging – you may want daily content for your blog because the traffic it generates leads to more opt in subscribers, and ultimately, higher profit margins when you have products to sell to your list.

You might use two areas of automation for this one task. First, you outsource the writing to a freelance ghostwriter. And second, you use the built in scheduler tool on WordPress to post the blog for you. There are even tools that can add the blog link and message to social media accounts for you.

Not all of the blogging process is automated. You still do the brainstorming, add your unique personalization to the content, and upload the item to your blog. But even those can eventually be automated if you find your own talents to be more profitable when you focus on product creation and let a virtual assistant handle the daily blog tasks.

Don't be afraid to let go of control of your business. It's a necessary part of the growth process. Find people and tools that you can trust – and don't be afraid to replace them if you find they're not working for you.

To Your HAPPINESS & SUCCESS!

THINK RIGHT ~ DO RIGHT ~ BE RIGHT!

DO IT NOW!

ABOUT THE AUTHOR

Edward Spade is an entrepreneur with decades of executive leadership and corporate consulting experience. He has a passion to help others succeed and is actively pursuing this through information marketing and providing others with tools and techniques to get their message and products out to the world.

"I've found that **Thinking Right** is one of the keys to developing your **Personal Greatness**. Everyone can improve themselves, their family, and their business."

"The process to be a better parent, a better friend, a better spouse or to earn more money is simple. **Train your mind** to find the good in every situation. See your problems as opportunities. When a bad thought enters your mind **Zap it out Immediately!**"

"**Take control of your mind** by *changing the input*. Input equals output. Change what you watch. Change what you listen to. Don't spend your time foolishly, instead *invest it wisely* in **the Future you**. This is the process by which your dreams are turned into reality."

THINK RIGHT ~ DO RIGHT ~ BE RIGHT...

DO IT NOW!